RALPH
NADER'S
CRUSADE

By the author of

THE LIFE OF MALCOLM X

RALPH NADER'S CRUSADE

Richard Curtis

MACRAE SMITH COMPANY
Philadelphia

Copyright © 1972 by Richard Curtis

Library of Congress Catalog Card Number 72–4379
Manufactured in the United States of America

Published simultaneously in Canada by George J. McLeod, Ltd.

ISBN 0–8255–2794–5

SECOND PRINTING

Acknowledgements

For her assistance in the preparation of this book, my deep appreciation goes to Martha Reeves, a hard worker, a dedicated conservationist, and a beautiful person.

3/935

For Bette Hogan and her Muz.

And for A. L. R.

RALPH NADER'S CRUSADE

CHAPTER

1

In March of 1966, a few weeks before the cherry blossoms of the nation's capital were to burst into bloom, a lanky young man with dark hair and grim eyes approached the ivory façade of the Old Senate Office Building. His pace was rapid, for he was late for a hearing with Senator Ribicoff and an unusual cast of characters. Nevertheless, he stopped to talk to the security guard as he entered the building.

"I guess this is the showdown," the man said, laughing.

"Yes, thanks to you," replied Ralph Nader. Ralph owed this guard a great deal, for it was he who had spotted the men who had been following Nader for several weeks and confirmed Ralph's suspicions that he was being tailed. The guard's tipoff had triggered a series of events that were to climax at today's hearing and cast Ralph Nader into the national limelight.

He passed into the high-ceilinged, echoing corridors and into the vaulted Senate Caucus Room where the Senate Subcomittee on Auto Safety was holding its hearing. James Roche, president of the world's largest nongovernment corporation, was already testifying. Senator Ribicoff, Senator Robert Kennedy, and other committee members, as well as a group of witnesses and representatives of the press, were listening intently to him, but the proceedings halted abruptly the moment Ralph Nader stepped into the room.

Tension rose almost palpably as camera crews focused their lights on the modestly dressed, slightly round-shouldered figure. For a second he seemed lonely and lost, but then he pulled himself up straight as he remembered that this was no talky, tedious, do-nothing hearing. No, this was a critical moment in history: the head of a billion-dollar company, General Motors, was apologizing publicly to a private citizen it had offended.

Ralph Nader was that citizen.

Seven months earlier, when his book *Unsafe at Any Speed* was published, he had had no inkling that such an event would, or even could, take place. Though the book's contents were sensational, its sales could scarcely be called that. In fact, it had caused only a mild ripple. Ralph's disappointment had been bitter. He couldn't believe the American public could be indifferent to the problem of automobile safety once the facts had been exposed. Almost everyone he spoke to knew

12

of someone who had been hurt, maimed, or even killed in an automobile accident of which mechanical failure, not driver error, had been the fault. Ralph himself had a close friend who had been crippled in a crash.

On another level, the book's lack of impact meant that he might have to continue as a salaried government employee, keeping him from the kind of work he really wanted to do—the kind that had resulted in *Unsafe at Any Speed*. He wanted to carry the theme of that book—that the industry often cares more about sales than safety—into other areas of American life, such as the food and drug industries. But it had seemed to him after the publication of his book that public apathy was going to defeat him.

Unknown to him, his book had irritated some people in the management of certain automobile manufacturers. In particular, his criticism of General Motor's Corvair, though grounded in solid and frightening fact, had pricked the tender skin of a few of that company's executives. They had decided to find out more about the author in the hope of discovering information they could use to discredit him. They'd therefore engaged detectives to dig into Ralph's background and life style. And dig they did, but when they came to the bottom of their excavations and sifted through every grain of his career, they had to admit there was nothing there to smear him with. He led a clean, quiet life; he appeared to have no vices; he had done nothing to be ashamed of, nothing he would want covered up; and he had no axe to grind. That is, he had no vested interest in attacking GM other than saving the lives and limbs of people who drove in its cars. He was not, as they had perhaps hoped to learn, being paid by one of GM's competitors to attack GM.

This frustrating lack of spicy information had only served to stimulate the investigators to try harder. They had begun following Ralph; and, Ralph was to assert later, they had even persuaded a girl to make advances towards him to see what kind of sex life he led. She had tried to pick him up in a supermarket. He had declined, but at the time it had not occurred to him to wonder whether she might have been planted for some insidious reason.

Before this incident, Ralph had merely had a slightly uneasy feeling that he was being watched. Then some of his friends phoned to tell him that people had come and asked questions about him. But when the guard at the Old Senate Office Building told Ralph he was certain Ralph was being followed, it was clear to him at once that this harrassment had something to do with the book. When his counterinvestigation had revealed that General Motors was behind it, Ralph had complained to some influential men in Washington, and they had helped him bring the matter to the attention of Congress and the public. The GM inquiry into Ralph Nader's private life backfired, causing its president acute embarrassment.

As Ralph took his seat, Senator Ribicoff looked at him and said, with an ironic twinkle in his eyes, "We're glad to see you finally made it. Mr. Roche was just saying something very interesting."

"I'm sorry I'm late," Ralph replied, his own eyes

seeming to kindle. "It's times like today when you can't get a cab that I'm tempted to buy a car. Maybe even a Chevrolet."

The laughter in the room eased tensions for a few moments, but then Senator Ribicoff solemnly indicated that Mr. Roche could continue making his statement.

James Roche was spare and gray-headed. He looked more like a college professor than the president of a giant corporation. He also looked acutely ill at ease.

He cleared his throat. "Let me make clear at the outset that I deplore the kind of harrassment to which Mr. Nader has apparently been subjected." He paused as a murmur rippled across the room. No one could remember when anything like this had occurred in the national capital.

"I am just as shocked and outraged by some of the incidents which Mr. Nader has reported as the members of this subcommittee. I did not know of the investigation when it was initiated and I did not approve it. . . . I am not here to excuse, condone or justify in any way our investigating Mr. Nader. To the extent that General Motors bears responsibility, I want to apologize here and now to the members of the subcommittee and Mr. Nader. I sincerely hope that these apologies will be accepted. Certainly I bear Mr. Nader no ill-will."

It took several minutes to quiet the room. For, in that frenzied space of time a number of things had become apparent. The first was that the head of a giant corporation had admitted that he was out of touch with what was going on in his business. The

15

second was that he had admitted that a smear campaign had been mounted against a critic of his company, implying that that critic must possess the power to hurt that company. Third, and above all: a new leader was born.

What was it that made this moment so magical? It was the stirring sight of a single man surmounting gigantic odds, recalling the frontier legends—the Lone Ranger ideal—on which our national pride was built. It was the inspiring fact that in an increasingly cynical world the truth still had the power to bring dishonest forces to their knees. The pen was still mightier than the sword. It was the encouraging spectacle of a super-technology—thought by most to be invulnerable and uncontrollable—brought to a halt, if only for one instant in time, and made to examine its conscience. There was something Biblical about it; people began talking about the new David who had dared to hurl a stone at the modern Goliath.

Still, no one, including Ralph Nader himself, foresaw the events that would follow this stunning victory, foresaw that issues that had quietly been bubbling beneath the surface of American life would erupt volcanically, affecting such diverse areas of our lives as the chemicals in our food, the filth in our air, the hazards in our mines, and the ineptitudes in our government. No one foresaw that before long Ralph Nader would be heading an informal but potent organization with a budget of over a million dollars. No one foresaw that Ralph Nader would soon be symbolizing for millions of Americans a host of virtues that were thought to have been lost: integrity, honesty, individualism, industriousness, simplicity, courage.

But more importantly, no one could ignore what was to come.

CHAPTER

2

The ten-room white clapboard house in Winstead, Connecticut, was right across the street from the county courthouse. When Ralph Nader was only four, he used to go across the street, sometimes to see his father in the family restaurant, sometimes to listen to the arguments in the courthouse. The lawyers quickly became used to seeing the skinny kid with the shock of dark hair and the huge dark eyes, sitting in the back corner, listening.

Ralph was fascinated with the happenings in the courthouse and with the arguments that flew back and forth. Even at that age he asked his father, "What do the lawyers do? What does the court do?"

To which his father would reply, "There are lawyers and lawyers. Sometimes they could do a lot. But most of the time they only do what their clients want them to, not necessarily what is right."

From his father, Ralph learned that the legal profession was one of the most powerful in the world, because a lawyer could change society.

Ralph Nader was born on February 27, 1934, the youngest of four children. His older sisters, Laura and Claire, and his brother, Shafik, were very congenial. Laura recalls that Ralph was the family comic. "He was always playing on words and getting us to laugh," she recalls, "especially at supper."

Ralph's parents were Lebanese. When they came to the sleepy Connecticut town of Winstead, his father opened his restaurant right across the street from their house. Ralph's father was something of a crusader himself. He would take cases to court without a lawyer, for the sake of the cause, just to fight for his rights, even when he was quite sure he would lose. And he was never too tired from his seven-day-a-week job to talk about the case at suppertime.

Ralph's mother was equally energetic. She had a consuming passion for her children and made sure that they always had something constructive to do. She noted which movies were in town. The Naders could not afford many movies, but when one came that had some purpose or message, she let the children go. Once, when the town was flooded by heavy rains, she organized all the mothers in the neighborhood to make sure that the children had something to do that was interesting and fun.

An unspoken family rule was that the Naders never lost their sense of being world citizens, and Americans as well. When Ralph was three, his parents took the family on a trip to Lebanon. The archbishop came to visit, and everyone kissed his hand. But when the archbishop reached Ralph, the small boy looked up at the large man and said, "I don't have to kiss your hand. I'm an American."

On their return, Ralph spoke Arabic better than English, and he didn't stop there. By the time he reached college he spoke five languages, including Russian and Chinese.

When it was time for little Ralph to begin school, the principal was worried about his English word skill and wanted to hold him back, but Ralph's parents refused, and they were right. All through grade school Ralph was always in the top of his class, though not just to be cooperative, or because he wanted to win. Good scholarship was simply what his family expected of him and what he expected of himself.

In the third grade, the future crusader became interested in nature. For one of his class projects he read all he could find about the great American naturalist John Muir and gave a talk on Muir's achievements to the class. Muir was a farsighted scientist who knew, even in the nineteenth century, how interdependent living things are on one another, and how fragile that balance is. He was one of the first to propose national parks. One of them, Muir Woods, a preserve of giant redwoods near San Francisco, was named after him. Ralph never forgot Muir or his early experience talking about him.

Life in Winstead was happy and fairly quiet. There were woods to walk in, and baseball and football after school. But Ralph was more likely to be found with his nose in a book than in a scrimmage. He was a good athlete, but he was also a bookworm and could read with fantastic speed.

This thirst for knowledge was one of several traits characteristic of the whole Nader family. All four children were exceptionally successful students. Never rich, his sister Laura recalls, the Naders had two amusements: talking and reading. Dinner would often last five hours, beginning at six-thirty and lasting until well after eleven.

Three influences from Ralph's childhood stayed with him and emerged when he became the nation's leading consumer advocate. One was his knowledge of and feeling for law, which came from his hanging around the local courts. The second was his experiences with the restaurant business. He visited his father's place often as a child and later worked there summers. The knowledge he gained was useful later in fighting poor food quality and danger in food products in the sixties and seventies.

The third, and probably most important thing, was his concern for people as individuals. Although he was shy at parties, Ralph always made friends easily, from the janitor in college to the head of his department. This trait grew out of the friendliness of the home-town people. As his sister Laura puts it, "When he sees that 50,000 people die in auto accidents, he doesn't see a number. He sees 50,000 individual people."

As Ralph grew, so did his fascination with lawyers and the legal profession. It was a dismal day for him when he first learned that lawyers would work for whoever paid them and did not always work for what was true and just. Ralph felt that a lawyer should serve people's needs, be more than merely a paid lobbyist in court or in Congress, and follow his conscience.

The word "lobbyist" was one he learned at an early age at the dinner table. He discovered that lobbyists were people paid by special-interest groups to influence public officials in their policy decisions. Many lawyers were directly engaged in lobbying or else politically active in an indirect way.

The more Ralph found out about the legal profession, the angrier he got—not with a rage that everyone could see, but with a growing conviction inside that by his own admission became an obsession. Very early he decided to become a lawyer, not because he admired his friends at the courthouse, but because he wanted to show people what the legal profession could really be like.

The definition of the word "advocate" had a lot to do with his ideal. An advocate is someone who defends a cause before a judge or a court. Ralph felt that there were a lot of things that had been neglected by advocates, including the defense and pleading of the cause of truth and honesty in the form of reliable products that would not kill, maim, damage or cheat the purchaser.

Ralph's desire to become a lawyer was encouraged by his parents. His mother never protested when he went to the courthouse. And, he says, "My father used to tell me what lawyers *could* do compared to what they *did* do. He took a very public-spirited view of things, and I learned that the legal profession was the most flexible, most catalytic spot from which to try to improve society."

After Ralph graduated from high school, he entered Princeton. There the English department made him take a remedial course in the language he felt he knew as well as any other, but he did not object too much. After all, an exact knowledge of English is very important to a legal education, where the precise connotation of a word can mean winning or losing a case.

But there were a lot of things he did not like about Princeton. All through school he had become increasingly dissatisfied with the educational process. The emphasis seemed to be on learning not for its own sake but for getting ahead in life. The goal of getting something and going somewhere was pounded into the student by school and society. You should learn to work for an economy ruled by huge corporations, a student was taught. Make money. Acquire possessions.

At Princeton he met a lot of students who lived by these principles. They wore identical clothes and spoke the same language. They were interested only in their clubs and the contacts they made there.

To these students, friends were important mainly because they would be useful in the future when they became successful. Everything else was approached in the same way: for its usefulness.

The Princeton campus was quite lovely, with its ivy-covered walls and tree-lined walks. Wilson Hall was a favorite study place of Ralph's, but it was locked too early to suit him. Ralph liked to study until three or four in the morning, so when he found the hall locked, he resorted to his ingenuity.

Finding a bathroom window on the ground level that was never locked, he made his entrances to the hall that way, until one night he came upon a startled professor after hours. After Ralph had explained himself, the professor got permission for him to have his own key to the hall. When Ralph's friends found out about the key, they tried to bribe him to let them use it to take their dates there. He refused, but not because he was a prude; it was simply the principle of the thing.

Ralph had many true friends at Princeton, and he accepted enough of the University's idea of education to get himself into law school. In his usual thorough way, he graduated *magna cum laude* with a Phi Beta Kappa key, among the highest scholastic awards one can receive. But he had found the educational process very depressing.

Never a dreamer, Ralph did not expect Harvard Law School to be much different. And it wasn't. "It was the worst conceivable distortion of legal education," he recalled later. "They were training us to be experts in servicing big businesses. In the meantime, the problems of the cities were building up, racial problems were building up, environmental problems were building up, bureaucracies were building up. And we weren't even exposed to these as challenges to our profession."

The one-sidedness of Harvard's attitude toward law did not discourage him. As a realist he was able to see that the problems around him were going to increase explosively. He saw the cheating that went on in industry and government. And while his classmates were busy hitting the books, he began to explore areas that he would later make his life's work.

"It's incredible," one of his law classmates said to another in front of the law library on the Harvard campus. "He never seems to study. He either knows it already or learns by osmosis. The type seeps through the book covers into his mind when he holds them!"

What the classmate did not know was that Ralph was already putting eighteen to twenty hours a day into his work. Always something of a night owl, he spent his days, when he was not in class, exploring areas of law with which few people were concerned.

For example, there were the Indians. Little had been done for their plight when Ralph was in law school. His sister Laura, who was an anthropologist, suggested that he see the situation for himself, and one summer he did. He was appalled at the administration of the reservations, at the horrible conditions under which they lived, with poor housing, little water, and barren land that would hardly support agriculture, sheep or cattle. Most of all, he was upset by the psychological state of the Indians. Because they felt that there was little use in protesting or trying to fight the Government's Indian Bureau, the rates of alcoholism and suicide among them were very high.

After returning from his depressing summer, Ralph

wrote a paper for the *Harvard Law Record* blasting the government for mismanagement and exposing the whole pitiless system under which Indians were living. The *Record* received thousands of requests for reprints of the article, but Ralph was too busy to enjoy this distinction. He had already begun his next project.

Ralph's objections to Harvard Law School were not confined to its overemphasis on corporate law. He found that there was little criminal law, Consumer law or environmental law being taught. Few courses were designed to help a lawyer serve the people. Most would serve the purposes of big businesses and government. "I wasn't anti-business then," Ralph once told a friend, "and I'm not anti-business now. I'm just pro-people."

And it was this concern that led him to do a paper on automobile safety during his senior year at Harvard Law School.

In spite of the promise that his Phi Beta Kappa key had symbolized, Ralph did not make the *Harvard Law Review*. That did not matter, however; he was too busy doing his own thing. He was known around campus as the "Lone Lebanese." But the Lone Lebanese was not standing still. He had read the Cornell University reports on automobile safety, stating how dangerous American cars were, so he began to read trade and engineering magazines. He sought more information from the companies themselves. And the companies unwittingly antagonized Ralph until automobile safety became an obsession.

When Ralph decided to write on automobile safety during his senior year at Harvard, he got in touch with industry public relations people. They were very smooth, very nice, and very uninformative. One company even went so far as to invite him to their plant. When he got there, he was given a standard public tour. Guides did not answer his questions. They treated him as if he were just another member of the ignorant public. The automobile industry then was king and let everyone know it. This made Ralph furious, and he decided not to rest until he had found out what was the real story on the automobile industry.

He attended classes less and less. It seemed that some Harvard professors taught by rote in the too-large classes. They weren't interested in his concerns, and worst of all, they seemed to be at least fifteen years out of touch with what was going on.

So he doggedly continued his research. He remembers a conversation with a truck driver when he was hitching a ride in his Princeton days.

"Is it always this rough?" he had asked the jouncing driver.

"Yeah," the driver replied, "and it gives me one big backache."

"Ever had kidney trouble?" asked Ralph, remembering an article he'd read somewhere.

"Sure," replied the truck driver. "Most of us drivers have it. It's the breaks of the game."

But Ralph did not think it had to be the breaks of the game. His ever-questioning mind asked why. As he continued hitching to find out more, he discovered other safety hazards. Drivers often hung coat hangers at the back of the truck cabs, where there was a hook. He suspected that the hook and hanger would go right through a driver's skull if there was an accident. He asked many drivers if that hook and hanger had to be in that place for a special reason. The answer was always no. That got him thinking even more about cars and their design.

All through school his wanderings continued. Sometimes his friends thought this activity was a little weird, but actually there was direction and purpose in it.

"Bet you won't get on the first truck that comes along!" a friend dared at one point.

"Bet I will," replied Ralph, "and if I take you up on it, you have to come along."

The first truck was headed for South Carolina. The friend was horrified but had to go along. When they reached the truck's destination, the friend took the first ride back north, but Ralph decided to stay and see the town. He was back in school by Monday morning.

Why this insatiable curiosity? Partly because Ralph Nader has an incredible gift for observing details like the dangerous hooks in truck cabs. While he was still a student at Princeton—years before *Silent Spring*, Rachel Carson's exposé of the chemical poisoning of the environment, was published—he noticed birds lying dead beneath some trees. That morning he and some other students had accidentally been sprayed by tree-sprayers using DDT. The students had been burned by the insecticide; the birds had been killed by it. "Why," he thought, "do birds and people have to suffer like this?"

The sight of the dead birds moved him enough to

28

write a letter to the Princeton daily newspaper, which ignored his protest. The editors had more important things on their minds.

Ralph's pity for the birds—and for his fellow students —was merely a sign of what was to follow. The research on automobile safety continued. Ralph rode trucks, read technical journals, and came up with an article entitled, "American Cars: Designed for Death," which was published in the *Harvard Law Record*.

Though it may seem that Ralph had little else to do but run around the countryside, the fact was that his family's financial situation was very difficult. Hurricane Diane destroyed his father's restaurant, and Ralph's older brother had to drop out of law school so that Ralph could continue in school. Ralph never forgot this.

"Among other things," his former roommate Edward Levin remembers, "—aside from being in the top half of his class, that is—Ralph spent all of his time working for money when he wasn't investigating to satisfy his curiosity. He ran an import business and managed a bowling alley. He could go for fifty or sixty hours and then be O.K. and ready for more after twelve hours of sleep. We never talked about the trivial stuff—it was always politics, cases, world affairs. But he was always a loner. Very few people could get through to him."

Ralph was far from being oblivious to pleasure, however. He liked to eat.

"There was this 'All You Can Eat' place near campus," Levin relates. "Ralph could go through more food than you'd think possible. He could easily run through a pound of sliced beef at a meal and then follow it with fruit and sweets. He hated processed food even then, and instead ate quantities of fish and salads. You should have seen the face of the restaurant proprietor when Ralph walked in. He grimaced!"

That particular restaurant featured enormous strawberry shortcakes. Someone once made Ralph a bet that he could not eat six of them, but a person does not bet idly with Ralph. He ate six of them and probably could have eaten more.

Ralph's rebellious spirit kept him going at Harvard, although occasionally it took a peculiar twist. Like the time he showed up for the wrong exam and got a high mark in a course he never even signed up for. It also kept him from going crazy in his two-year Army stint. The Army, in its infinite wisdom, made Ralph—with his ability to work twenty hours a day and his almost inexhaustible brain and photographic memory—a cook.

Ralph kept up his poking around the automobile industry. And finally, when a friend was made a paraplegic in an automobile accident, the die was cast.

CHAPTER

3

Ralph's Harvard article on automobile safety, "American Cars: Designed for Death," caused a flurry in the legal profession, and the *Harvard Law Record* was deluged with requests for reprints.

Ralph continued to watch keenly what was going on in the industry, for what had begun as curiosity had now developed into something akin to a compulsion.

After Harvard he took off on a short journalistic career, writing travel articles for newspapers from Europe, the Middle East, and Russia. One of his articles appeared in *The New York Times*. However, he soon ended his wanderings and returned home to pursue his legal career.

He was interested in an article by Daniel Patrick Moynihan, later to become one of the top men in the

Nixon Administration, on highway safety. Moynihan was concerned that the tire industry's product was so shoddy that it contributed to thousands of highway deaths every year. The substance of the article was that the industry had better shape up before someone clamped strict regulations on it.

Ralph wrote to Moynihan, and the traffic safety expert was impressed with the young lawyer's writing and work. They kept in touch for several years, and when Moynihan took a job with the Kennedy Administration, he invited Ralph to come to Washington. Moynihan thought that the auto safety problem really belonged in the Department of Public Health, but, he has commented, "That was a dead bureaucracy that was incapable of even comprehending the problem."

Both Moynihan and Ralph were working in the Department of Labor. Moynihan was Assistant Secretary of Labor, and Nader worked as a follow-up man. "He was intense and competent and available," recalls Moynihan. "He understood what I was talking about. . . . He was most effective in getting others interested. He went over to the Department of Justice all the time to convince them that there was an element of restraint of trade involved here."

For a time it seemed that they were beating their heads against a brick wall. But suddenly a scandal broke. It was discovered that the director of a government committee on automobile safety was receiving money from the automobile industry. This reflected not only on the committee but also on the Administration itself.

Finally Moynihan and Nader had something to go on. But proof of collusion was not enough. Ralph continued to expand the knowledge he had picked up in hitching around the country. It was "Nader's genius," Moynihan said later, "that was to discover that cars were just not designed well and were not built well, and that they could be."

Ralph became so wrapped up in his project that he left the Department of Labor to write a book. He worked on it seven days a week, eighteen hours a day. He pored over technical journals, auto magazines, and legal documents, and finally, in 1965, *Unsafe at Any Speed* was published, dedicated to his friend who had suffered severe injury and paralysis as a result of an accident due to faulty engineering. Ralph's book was not the only one on the subject. The same season brought Jeffrey O'Connell's *Safety Last.* The O'Connell book was better written, it was generally agreed, but Nader's had the technical information and the legal expertise. It was not O'Connell but Nader whom General Motors sought to expose. The book was the last straw for the industry, which had been watching Ralph closely during his service with Moynihan.

In January of 1966, a firm of private investigators was hired by General Motors attorney Richard Danner. Although the investigators later made protestations of good will at the Senate hearings that followed this tawdry episode, their instructions to the team had read in part, "The above applicant is a free lance writer and attorney. Recently he published a book called *Unsafe at Any Speed,* highly critical of the automobile industry's interest in safety. Our client apparently made some cursory inquiry into Nader to determine his expertise, interest, background, backers if any. They found out relatively little about him, and that little is detailed below. Our job is to check his life and current activities, to determine what makes him tick, such as his real interest in safety, his supporters, if any, his politics, his marital status, his friends, his women, boys, drinking, dope, jobs, in fact all facets of his life."

But this cynical report and directive was not enough to determine what made Ralph tick.

Although it was never made clear what GM told the investigators to do, they apparently were not out to prove whether or not Ralph was qualified in automobile design and engineering. They were out to find any dirt they could about him, including whether he was anti-Semitic; whether he had girl friends, and if so who they were and what his relationship with them was; and by whom, if anyone, Ralph was being paid to do his work.

From the testimony at the Senate committee hearings, it is obvious that the investigators bungled the job. They put a tail on Ralph. When their investigation got nowhere, the investigators, not knowing that Ralph had an office, had the brilliant idea of calling his home address.

"He lives here," said the landlady, "but he's not in at the moment."

Stimulated by this success, the investigators then decided to try to find out if Ralph owned a car. They made a trip to New Hampshire to interview Frederick

34

Hughes Condon, to whom Ralph had dedicated his book, but they could not get the information they wanted.

They also could not understand the information they had. Unable to believe that anyone would live as monkish a life as Ralph, they tried to find out about his private social activities. No one has been less successful than they. In his protest filed with the Senate committee, Ralph claimed that the investigators had used girls as "bait" to try to prove there was an immoral side to his character. At the committee hearings, the investigators denied engaging in such activities. Perhaps the whole truth will never be known.

At the Senate hearings, Ralph testified that he was being harassed. The investigators, he said, were investigating all aspects of his personal life, talking to his teachers, friends and business associates. Strange girls accosted him in the supermarket, and he was followed everywhere. It was getting on his nerves and interfering with his work. Above all, it proved that industries such as GM would go to great lengths to hinder his own investigations.

The investigations, which had cost General Motors $6,700, were an embarrassment to the corporation. Its president made the apology quoted in the first chapter of this book, and at the end of the hearings, tired and embarrassed, he made a final statement: "It will not be our policy in the future to undertake investigation of those who speak or write critically of our products."

After the hearing had adjourned, however, the investigators seemed to feel no embarrassment. One of them went up to Ralph and introduced his wife. "I could have saved you a lot of trouble. All you had to do was ask," said Ralph, pulling out his driver's license. The investigator actually copied the number down.

It is clear that the investigation was more than routine and did constitute a determined effort to smear Ralph. But the bungling investigators had been seeking a trail that did not exist. In the cynical atmosphere of Washington, no one understood Ralph. "Is this guy for real?" was the common reaction. The investigators could not believe that Ralph was exactly what he represented himself to be.

Ralph was so resentful of GM's harassment that he filed suit against the company and the investigators at the end of 1966. The suit dragged on for four years and in 1970 was settled in Ralph's favor. He had sued for $26,000,000, but ended up with only a half million. The money went immediately into his work.

Although Ralph had done some consultant work before the Senate hearings, at the time he was supported by no one but himself. He ironically points out that *Unsafe at Any Speed* was hardly a bestseller and had sold only 26,000 copies at the time of the furor. The book has since been reissued, and the 1972 edition is updated and revised.

Ralph is one of those rare men who can be taken at face value. "People are funny," he has said, not without irony. "They tolerate a rebel with a cause, but not one with a remedy. It's all right in America for someone to speak out, but if he becomes successful, watch out."

In *Unsafe at Any Speed,* Ralph had cited innumerable dangerous features in the Corvair: the steering column would impale the driver in a left-front collision. The dashboard was a death trap for anyone thrown against it. The rear-end suspension was dangerously unbalanced and would easily throw a car into a spin or a rollover. This was part of the rebel's cause.

The solution was an emphasis on safety by government as well as industry. The industry could stop emphasizing speed, reduce car fatigue by changing design, improve the driver's view, cut out dangerous ornaments, and improve headlights. Government could promote better laws and enforcement, insist on driver education, and require periodic inspection of cars. These were but a few of the faults and remedies that the rebel proposed.

And what did Ralph think of GM, whose president before the hearings had not even known of the investigation that had caused an individual such personal harassment?

"I criticize a system where the man at the top has no communication with the bottom, where the man in the middle does what he thinks will please and the man down below does only what he is told." This, in Ralph's opinion, is an atmosphere in which automobile safety is the last feature to be attended to.

All through the auto safety battle, Ralph's equanimity was undisturbed. "What sustains me," he said, "is the knowledge that I can't win but at least I'll be able to civilize things a bit more."

The Senate hearings ended in February, and in March Ralph resigned from his law practice to devote himself full-time to the automobile safety problem.

By the end of 1966, the first bills on automobile safety had been passed, but Ralph remarked that it would not be until the seventies that any significant changes would show. "The automobile industry built bumpers on cars," he quipped, "and then built on bumper guards to protect the bumpers."

Ralph found that he could not end his investigations with automobile safety. He became involved in research into pollution as a by-product of that concern, and that led him into other areas, including the meat-packing industry. It was on one of his many trips to universities to speak that he first had the idea of establishing a public interest law firm.

By that time, of course, Ralph had achieved fame, if not notoriety, in some circles. Many people in the automobile industry still were watching him like a hawk to see if he would stray from the straight-and-narrow way of life.

He continued to live in his $80-a-month flat in a boarding house, and still does. "I hate to raise the rent," his landlady said in 1971. "By now everyone knows how much he pays; it's almost an institution."

Ralph works seven-day weeks, eighteen hours a day. He does not smoke or drink, except for an occasional glass of wine. He refuses to eat sugar, salted nuts, or anything with artificial ingredients or additives that he thinks might be dangerous. He still has a sweet tooth and often consumes two desserts at a meal, but the practice has had little effect on his tall, lanky, frame.

Part of the reason for this is that he is always on the run. One-night stands are the order of the day, and when he gets home at night he reads and studies and writes until all hours of the morning. He survives on about four hours of sleep a night and has few amusements. As a child he could quote most of the major league batting averages, but although he still follows baseball in the papers, he never goes to games, watches television, or goes to the movies.

Work is his meat, drink, and entertainment. Each day he reads at least half a dozen papers and trade journals, works with his staff of "raiders," and often also testifies before a committee or fills a speaking engagement. He is a compulsive telephone user.

He wants no fame for himself, and while he supports himself by giving lectures and writing, the bulk of the $200,000 a year or so that he earns goes to support the "raiders," his public-interest law projects, and other activities related to consumer law. He refuses autographs, tries to travel anonymously, and declines all offers to involve him in politics, which, he says, would immediately compromise the whole idea.

With this record, it is no wonder that the investigators joined the "Is this guy for real?" crowd of disbelievers. To maintain such a schedule, sometimes making six speeches a day, is a killing task in itself. In one day Nader often works on at least six different projects, making notes and telephone calls, and driving his colleagues to heights of performance they never knew they could reach.

He can be abrupt with waiters and waitresses. At a

now-legendary lunch in Washington, D.C., he found a dead fly in his chef's salad. In a rage he sent it back, and while waiting for the substitute to come harangued his companions on the subject of the gross violations of sanitary laws and health and safety codes that exist in many restaurants.

When the waiter brought him a new salad, Ralph looked suspiciously under every leaf, and when dessert arrived he asked the flustered waiter, "Any flies in this?"

"I hope not, sir," came the reply.

"Well," rejoined Ralph, "if there's any doubt, take it away." The waiter hastily reassured Ralph, who then finished his meal.

But Ralph also has a sense of humor. Sometimes it tends to be on the morbid side, but then he is often dealing with morbid subjects. For instance, when it comes to their ability to stand up against the impact of accidents, he has likened foreign cars to "Japanese lanterns." On the occasion of a speech in Tulsa, Oklahoma, a big oil city, the microphone failed. It didn't faze Ralph. He merely said, "If I were as paranoid as the oil industry I'd think that was a conspiracy," and pushed on with his speech.

When addressing an audience he will always give basically the same speech, abundantly illustrated with facts and figures. While his speaking style includes a lot of *um*'s and *ah*'s, he still manages to magnetize his audience.

When Ralph began to make the rounds of colleges in his first flush of fame, his ideas caught on. He urged students to conduct their own investigations in their local communities and to develop their critical faculties. "You should do as much work at the college level as you're able on problems you really care about. You must get out of your college libraries at times and work on local problems to which you have access. You must develop your critical abilities and do it in such a way that it makes you strain. Stress, strain and pressure are often the only ways to develop creative capacities."

1966 was the first big year for Ralph Nader's crusade. There were General Motors hearings, Ralph's involvement with automobile safety, and then the extension of his investigations into industrial pollution and the meat packing industry and the first inklings of his idea of a public law firm.

In 1966, also, came the first signs of a serious economic decline. Corporations began to marshal themselves against the inevitable attacks to come. The decline in the stock market had coincided with Ralph's testimony in the Senate, and many people irrationally blamed him for undermining confidence in the American economy. Actually, the slump was long overdue. The escalation of the Vietnam war had already begun an inflationary spiral that happened to make itself evident at the time Ralph first came into public view. This was partly a result of the unsuccessful attempt of the American economy after 1945 to switch from a wartime to a peacetime basis.

In 1967 Ralph consolidated his position as a consumer advocate, and by 1968 the idea of public law became a reality as the first six "raiders" began working

41

for him. At first these raiders were simply volunteers offering to lend assistance free of charge to a man whose cause they admired but whose funds were limited. Later, as more revenue came in and Ralph began to realize the scope of his investigation, he was able to expand his group of disciples and pay many of them for their work, albeit modestly. By 1969 there were 102 raiders, and the numbers continue to grow.

As one journalist put it in 1971, "Three years ago he was a one-man band. Now he's a conglomerate." Ironically, Ralph began to suffer from some of the same ills of the larger corporations whose mergers and geometric progressions of growth he thinks injurious to consumer and economy alike.

None of Ralph's raiders labor under any delusions that their work is glamorous. "The image is so far off!" one of them commented. "It's not the dashing young Cossack charging in and laying waste to the Establishment. It's working long hard hours, reading day after day what is boring—trivia, hearings, memos, letters, scholarly treatises. It's just hard, tedious work."

Nor is working for Nader likely to make a raider rich. "When you're working on policy questions, Ralph is open and reflective and encourages full participation," one has reported. "But boy, if you use too much Xerox paper, watch out."

Ralph does not consider himself a very tough taskmaster. "Whoever works hard with us," he has said, "works hard because he wants to, or she wants to. Whoever doesn't like to get pushed very much just doesn't get renewed, but that has happened very infrequently."

Ralph's example holds the whole thing together. "Somehow when he's around you don't bring up things like the fact that you have a backache. It doesn't seem proper." another raider has commented.

Ralph is not around very much. He leaves his raiders to do much of the legwork while he flies around the country making enough money to keep the operation going.

In several states students have raised enough money to finance their own consumer protection groups. But Ralph has bigger plans.

The nonprofit Center for the Study of Responsive Law got started with Ralph's own funding and support from foundations. As Chairman of its Board he receives no money for serving. The reports of the 102 students who worked for him in 1969 were bound together, and the royalties from the book, which came in part from them, have gone into the fund to subsidize further investigations.

Some of the books that are the outcome of the summer investigations are *Vanishing Air, The Chemical Feast,* and *The Interstate Commerce Omission.* Perhaps one of the most explosive studies was one done by a group of prep school girls on nursing home conditions.

In 1971 Ralph made his plans even more public. He took out a full-page ad in *The New York Times* and other periodicals outlining the need for public representation on a consumer basis. He asked people to contribute for their own good to his nonprofit organizations.

It is not yet clear how willing people are to part with money voluntarily to help keep corporations from taking it from them unknowingly. But Ralph is confident of success.

He has come to reject both the words "Advocate" and "Lobbyist." "We're developing and implementing a full-time career of citizenship," he says. "There must be a group in each profession—engineering, medicine, law—that represents what it thinks is the professional mission: safer machines, better medical care, better courts. What we are working for is a redeployment of manpower so that when lawyers represent corporations before the Federal Power Commission or the Federal Trade Commission, facing them will be lawyers who put the same full-time professional skill into representing what they think are the public interests. In time, I hope, ten thousand lawyers will get up in the morning to do just that."

Can Ralph Nader succeed? Does he overestimate the number of people willing to make the sacrifices he has imposed on himself, or is he a sort of prophet, who sees aright the signs of the times?

Only time will tell. Not everybody is willing to work for $35 to $100 a week, which is a raider's salary. But many have come to work for Ralph, and more express interest all the time.

Ralph sees a way out of the financial difficulties. "We're going to have to change our whole psychology

44

of philanthropy. Hundreds of thousands of dollars are now going into traditional charities with huge overheads that don't do anything more than put Band-aids on problems. Second, there are foundations—they might help. Third, I think more and more people would willingly give five or ten dollars a year to contribute to something that would really cause change. And fourth, I think that government will have to develop subsidies.

"Government is now paying salaries of 1,800 neighborhood legal service lawyers working in the slums. But more important, the government is now spending hundreds of millions of dollars on subsidies to business through oil-depletion laws and maritime and agri-business subsidies. We can make a much stronger case for the need to subsidize public defenders."

But Ralph faces more than the financial problems of keeping his nonprofit organizations going. How much longer can he physically stand the pace at which he works? There are few people in history who have been able to work and thrive on the schedule he keeps.

And is his idea of public interest law necessarily the right one? He has already parted company with several of the original raiders on the "right" way to develop consumer protection groups and lawyers to push for legislation.

Time alone will tell, but Ralph has somehow managed to be the right man in the right place at the right time.

CHAPTER
4

Why do some men make it and others not? Why does an issue that has been building up for years finally explode when one person arrives on the scene? Why was it Ralph Nader who set off the bomb of consumerism rather than one of the other crusaders who had been around for years?

Back in 1935 the nonprofit Consumer's Union began. The purpose of this private group is to test products, rank and grade them according to set standards, and make recommendations by brand name to its members. It tests products for their safety, price and reliability, and for their ability to do what they were intended and advertised to do. Consumer's Union split into Consumer's Union, which remained nonprofit and of which Ralph is a director, and *Consumer Reports,* a magazine, which began to advertise and make its reports commercially available while still forbidding products to advertise its ratings.

Consumers Union has a unique position in that it can not be accused of bias or operating for self-interest, since it does not receive money from the manufacturers of the products it tests.

Large as it has grown, Consumers Union has not in a real way accomplished what it set out to do, especially in areas of legislation. As long as it is a nonprofit organization, it has to walk a narrow path and refrain from actions that would be constituted as "political." This word can be interpreted in a number of ways. Filing suit against the government is one. Certain kinds of lobbying and pressures to influence decisions of public officials is another. If a nonprofit organization participates in these activities, it loses its nonprofit status and is subject to tax laws.

In its later years, *Consumer Reports* has itself become a huge enterprise. It concentrates on mass-media advertising to sell its magazine, although it still remains a nonprofit organization. It has also been joined on the market by other consumer-oriented magazines and newspapers, which now number in the hundreds. These publications vary from scandal sheets to reports of cooperatives in which a number of families band together to buy foodstuffs and other items at wholesale prices. These publications cover the whole range of consumer interests. But although they try to protect consumers they are in business for profit, for consumer protection is now big business.

There were other people before Ralph, and other books before *Unsafe at Any Speed*. Upton Sinclair's *The Jungle* exposed the repulsive conditions under which meat was packed in the earlier part of the century. *The Insolent Chariots* by John Keats exposed the duplicity of automotive advertising and the shoddy design and engineering of automobiles.

The Jungle caused quite a stir and led to some legislative reforms that were effective to a degree, but few of the other books led directly to legislation. While these books attacked problems, exposed attitudes, and made gray flannel suits very unpopular, they didn't have the combination of ingredients that Ralph and his book had.

Besides being the right person at the right time, Ralph had a better-than-average knowledge of several fields, from the restaurant and food industry to automobile engineering; an unusual, almost uncanny, sense of press timing; and total integrity.

The "right time" was partly a matter of accident. The American psychology had undergone profound changes since the second world war.

The United States created a lifestyle for itself that called for more of everything: more wealth, more possessions, more luxury, more comfort, more conveniences. An easily acquired taste for instant heat, instant food, and instant travel created a demand for still more products—new products. The word "new" became, and still is, one of the most powerful and often-used words in advertising.

But the rush toward an ideal of three cars in every

garage did not fulfill the American dream. Pursuing what looked like life, Americans found themselves embroiled in the Korean and Vietnamese wars. Instead of gaining liberty, the average American, by the mid-sixties, found that he had become a computer cipher, was in debt with time payments and frequently was a victim of private and corporate spying.

Even as early as the McCarthy era in the fifties, people began to wonder if their telephones were tapped. The credit industry began to keep files on all customers, as did the FBI and even the Army, on citizens it considered "suspect." Corporations tried to steal their rivals' secrets, and intricate information networks were set up in industry, using equipment that would make the CIA envious.

This was the situation in the early sixties, and Americans found themselves increasingly discontented. They were learning that "more" and "new" did not necessarily mean "right" and "better." They found that the transistor radio went dead three days after the guarantee ran out. The television needed frequent and expensive repair, and more often than not the repairman not only did not know his job but paved the way for future repairs on the set. The ad men made the consumer a fall guy who often did not get a penny's worth of value for a nickel.

Claims by advertisers for everything from mouthwashes to machine tools proved false. Nothing seemed to do what it claimed to do. Fortified breads and cereals were found to be nutritionally inadequate; housewares broke down and their guarantees were found to be worthless. Nothing lived up to expectations. A credibility gap developed between advertiser and consumer, which added to the general malaise of the country.

And the thought that one couldn't believe what one heard spread to other areas of life. Could you believe your employer, your parents, your government? Was your employer's profit that small? Were your parents' values right for you? Were the United States foreign involvements a good and honorable thing? Or were all of these things just more of the "We are better, we are best" attitude that much of the world, rightly or wrongly, had grown to suspect or even dislike?

Nevertheless many consumers still were falling, fell —and fall today—for advertising gimmicks. Though consumers are better educated and more sophisticated today than ever before, advertisers have become shrewder too. Earlier in this century, they used to say about a gullible person that you could sell him the Brooklyn Bridge. Today, one joke goes, few people would buy the Brooklyn Bridge—unless they could charge it on their credit cards.

Corporate malpractices are only half the battle for men like Ralph Nader. The other half is public apathy.

The source of such apathy is complex. In a world threatened by nuclear war, ungovernable science and technology, and social and political forces that change faster than our ability to comprehend them, there is a feeling that nothing we do makes a difference, that we are destined to bear the dehumanization of society stoically. Every moment of our day brings new assaults on human dignity. The morning ride to work on bus or train is about as pleasant as one in a cattle car. The streets of our cities subject us to deafening noise, poisonous fumes, and rude, indifferent people. Even at home our privacy is often battered by the racket coming through the thin walls of shoddily constructed buildings. There seems to be nowhere to turn—except perhaps the numbing monotony of the television tube.

Older people have become nostalgic for the days when—at least so it seems to them—hard work and honesty paid off, "fun" was simple and sincere, crime and lawlessness were exceptions rather than rules, "Yankee ingenuity" was admired and respected, and a dollar was worth a dollar. We know of course that none of these things is true, that in the past also we had financial depression, wars, social and political unrest, and turbulent technological change. Nevertheless, the nostalgia we are feeling is symptomatic of a national longing for honesty, simplicity, and dignity. In the absence of those values, we sink dejectedly into a state of apathy.

And so, by the midsixties, restless modern middle America was ready for a Ralph Nader. People were asking, "Why doesn't anything work any more? And why do I pay twice as much for it? If we can talk about putting men on the moon, why can't someone make an electric blender that lasts longer than six months?"

Pride in "Yankee ingenuity" was gone, too. Instead, "Made in Japan," a label that had once symbolized shoddy goods, had become a respected label of quality in electronics, textiles, optics and automobiles. Many Japanese products became more reliable than American ones, and not only American industry but American pride suffered.

Union unrest, rising production costs, more expensive raw materials, inflation, and constantly increasing defense budgets have made foreign products even more desirable.

Americans were further confused by the growth of conglomerates. While antitrust laws can keep corporations from taking over a particular product market, there is nothing on the books that says corporations cannot diversify and get into as many businesses as possible. Electronics companies bought book publishers and food giants bought tool companies.

With the acquisition of a new company often came the firing of the management. If you are fifty years old, have a family, have given ten years or so to a company and suddenly find yourself without a job, you begin to wonder if values like loyalty and hard work are worth it. It is hard to find a job when you are fifty.

But the biggest corporate backfire was caused by the classic practice of planned obsolescence. Technology has progressed far enough to enable a manufacturer to design a part for an automobile that will last for just so many miles and no more—or a refrigerator motor that will cool just so many hours and no more. After a period of time that has been carefully calculated by the manufacturer, the consumer is forced to buy a new article.

Government, too, began to get out of hand. It was already becoming apparent, when Ralph Nader came on the scene, that increasing taxes did not necessarily mean that community and government services would be delivered to communities. Regulatory agencies did not regulate. The bureaucracy became topheavy. Millions of dollars were lost in Federal programs.

With lack of regulation and growth of industry has come pollution, undrinkable water, unbreathable air, shrinking wilderness areas, and the permanent disappearance of certain wildlife.

In one of his speeches, Ralph put it this way: "The merger tide, unless abated, will leave us by 1975 with two hundred corporations holding seventy-five percent of all manufacturing assets. The largest of them all, General Motors, last year grossed more than the entire gross national product of Brazil—more than the gross receipts of any foreign government except the U.S.S.R. and Great Britain."

It is not only size, though, that represents a danger. Ralph goes on to tell how "Big Biology" can make George Orwell's "1984" look like nursery school.

"It is not inconceivable that the year 2000 will witness an announcement by Dupont that it can now produce a prototype man as part of its 'progress through chemistry.' And General Electric may declare that it at last can abolish night, an environmental enlightenment whose adoption is urged in order to reduce crime and traffic accidents. . . . The forces streaming out of our large corporations are changing the nature of the economy, altering the man-made environment to the point of mass crisis, and transforming our system of government."

The biological revolution, Ralph frequently points out, raises moral questions that are almost unsolvable

53

without drastic revision of our official moral code. "Who gets artificial hearts? When? Under what conditions and warranties? At what prices?"

Who does *not* get the artificial heart?

Who is allowed to die because he has been judged by others to be unfit?

Shouldn't people be granted the right to die in peace with a minimum of pain, instead of being plugged into computers, respirators and intravenous feeding machines that maintain life "with a maximum of discomfort and can keep a body alive long after life of any quality and/or awareness of anything but pain has long vanished?"

The capacity to solve such questions was up to now generally attributed to higher powers. Technology has long wrestled with nature for control of human destiny, and now that it has to a certain extent succeeded we do not know how to make these godlike decisions.

Ralph Nader's concern about the growth of large business corporations is more than simple concern about size and power. "Aside from the alleged benefits of such concentrations of corporate power," he asks, "what about the social costs of private, closed enterprise in such a monolithic framework? . . . What we do about corporate air and water pollution, corporate soil and food contamination, corporate-bred trauma on our highways, corporate lack of innovation or suppression of innovation, corporate misallocation of resources, corporate inflationary pricing, corporate dominance over local, state and federal agencies, and corporate distortions of political campaigning—to suggest a few issues —will decide our quality of life."

Throughout his career Ralph has had the ability to see the whole scope of the problems that interest him. This is one major reason why he caught the public's attention. A problem in his view is seldom one simple question to be answered. It is more likely a complex network of problems, requiring a variety of remedies.

One of the major aspects of corporation power on which Ralph has spoken out from the beginning is corporate deceit. "Large corporations . . . have deliberately refused to notify owners of defective vehicles, deliberately bilked the government of millions in inflated cost submissions under government contracts, negligently wasted millions of public funds in wasteful or promotional endeavors, without, in many cases, even resulting in sanctions and almost never in criminal penalties on the culpable offenders."

In other words—especially where the products concerned directly affect human welfare, automobiles and drugs, included—the corporations are literally getting away with murder. And in the process they are changing our natural and political environment so radically that by the time we become fully aware of the implications, it may be too late to stop what Ralph calls the corporate "Frankenstein."

Two interesting historical developments contributed to Ralph's prominence in the public view in 1966. Aside from the first big drop in the stock market around the time that he was in the Senate Office Building debating with General Motors, there was another, more gradual change. It was the growing concern and disillusionment of young people with the world their parents had created, culminating in the so-called "hippie" movement, the hard-drug culture, and the student riots of the late sixties.

The economic decline was long overdue. Industry had overestimated the volume of products consumers would buy and now had to cut back on production. During the boom of the past ten years, many companies had taken on too many employees. As soon as the demand for goods receded, these extra workers were let go. A number of specialized businesses, such as the aerospace industry, found their budgets cut drastically by the whim of Congress. This not only put some of the best-trained men in the country out of work but closed the door on employment to countless numbers of college graduates who had been encouraged to enter those very fields.

This bad economic turn increased the disaffection of our youth. Witnessing the emptiness of American materialism, the meaninglessness of traditional values, and the belligerence of American militarism, young people began to drop out of society by the thousands. Some sought refuge in communal experiments, drugs, religious cults, aimless travel, sexual excess, or simply anonymity. Others chose to try to change the values that had alienated them through public protest demonstrations and sometimes even through violence toward symbols of the Establishment leading to student strikes, protests and marches, and even more radical manifestations, including bombings and arson.

Thus America in the late sixties and at the turn of the decade was ripe for new leadership. Though the "generation gap" was much talked about, older and younger generations had a great deal in common. For both, the vaunted American Dream had turned into a nightmare. The older generation was beginning to realize that the values and virtues it had lived by, which still controlled the character and behavior of the nation, were somewhat hollow and absurd. The younger generation had never accepted those values and virtues to begin with, but it faced an entirely different problem: it did not have the power to change the character and behavior of the nation. All in all, the United States seemed to be undergoing a mammoth identity crisis.

It was in this atmosphere that Ralph Nader launched his campaigns. He had no trouble finding students to work for him. Although the new culture had produced many revolutionaries, it also had produced many reasonable individuals who believed that social problems could be solved by working within the American legal system. He attracted law students to work on legal problems, and set college and high school students to researching and interviewing.

He not only gave students work to do; he gave them a direction, a purpose, and a meaning. In his speeches he urged them to organize themselves into groups to investigate local problems of safety, pollution, and consumer fraud, if for no other reason than to protect themselves. In each address (he has only one basic speech which he embellishes with discussion of current issues that concern him) he tries to make clear the insidious dangers of corporate domination of economy and government and of technology that has gone out of control. He dissects problems and proposes cogent solutions; but most of all, and without really being aware of it, he presents himself as the model, the catalyst, the inspiration, the "way."

CHAPTER

5

The sporty blue car moved down the clear, dry highway at about thirty-five miles an hour. The driver was alert—it was about ten o'clock in the morning—and it was a bright and sunny day. He glanced in the rearview mirror to check traffic. There were three other cars in view, none of them within half a mile on that flat California highway. He turned on the radio to listen to his favorite country music disc jocky. There was a light spring wind blowing, gusting occasionally, but without serious force.

Suddenly one of those gusts, not more than twenty miles per hour, caught the blue car as it was going over a part of the road that had been roughened to give extra traction in rain. The car lurched crazily to the right, then to the left, and finally flipped over and skidded to a stop, enveloping the trunk of an old eucalyptus tree.

The driver was killed almost instantly. The left front wheel, almost a foot out of alignment, had sent the steering wheel through his chest.

Within minutes, the California highway patrol was on the scene. Two tough, highly-trained officers inspected the wreckage and called for an ambulance and a tow truck. They didn't say much to each other. When the twisted carcass of the auto was cleared away, the two patrolmen got back in their car and sat in silence. One of them raised his fist and slammed it down on the dashboard.

"That's the sixth one this month. I tell you, Dan, there's something wrong with the Corvair. I don't know if it's that rear engine or the crazy suspension, but that's six cars that shouldn't have been in accidents. And I'd be willing to bet the driver was sober."

Dan buckled his seat belt and drove toward Los Angeles. There was nothing to say. They could only report the accident and wait for it to happen again. And happen it did, many times.

After World War II, high horsepower and flashy design expressed the growing mood of devil-may-care driving. Models sported high, sharp fins, front hood ornaments that mutilated pedestrians, bumpers that crumpled at low speeds, and increasingly poor design in interiors and engines.

"Recall" was a word rarely heard in automobile circles before the midsixties. Manufacturers might send letters to dealers urging them to make necessary adjustments in defective cars, but they did not provide means for those dealers to get in touch with car owners, nor did they supply sufficient parts to cope with the defects.

The prevailing attitude up to that time was "It's the driver's fault," and this was the legal position taken by automotive manufacturers when the question of liability for accidents was raised. The Automotive Safety Foundation, for instance, recently quoted a tire mogul as saying, "Being inanimate, no car, truck or bus can by itself cause an accident any more than a street or highway can do so. A driver is needed to put it into motion —after which it becomes an extension of his will."

Statements like this, said Ralph Nader, are patently absurd. Picture an emergency brake kicking out of place by itself and the empty car careening down a hill to smash property and people. Certainly the car did not decide to become a runaway. In a sense the ASF is right: accidents are caused by people—but many times by the people who make the cars.

Someone made that defective brake, or that defective transmission, just as someone made the dangerous suspension in the Corvair's original design. Improperly placed rivets, screws left untightened, cylinders designed to give out after a certain number of miles— defective manufacture is indeed always due to human error, and it may take time to show itself, at terrible cost in life and limb. A combination of carelessness and so-called "planned obsolescence" has begun to make the American automotive industry an embarrassment to the nation.

When the Auto Safety Act of 1966 was passed, the event was a tremendous victory, not only for Ralph, but also for the tens of thousands of Americans driving cars that were destined to crash because of defects. It meant a major victory over the giants of the corporate establishment—a breach of their public relations fortifications and a complete turnabout of the old philosophy that accidents are always caused by drivers.

Unsafe at Any Speed and the resulting furor of publicity were primarily responsible for the passage of the act. In that book, Ralph cited an accident that had nearly brought the errors of GM and other manufacturers out in the open. A woman was driving under conditions similar to those in the accident described earlier. When her Corvair flipped, she lost an arm. Instead of chalking the disaster off as just another highway accident, she sued General Motors. The manufacturer took the case to court, but hastily settled out of court when the highway patrol and other experts gave their evidence.

At the time Ralph published his book (1965), the Corvair had been in production for five years. Designed to compete with smaller imported cars, the automobile was hazardous. Somehow GM escaped with a few settlements out of court and a minimum of bad publicity. The management quietly handed out a kit to repair the faulty rear suspension but made no effort to contact individual owners or recall the defective cars for replacement of the part.

Ralph did a lot of careful research for *Unsafe at Any Speed.* When it was published, he had enough ammunition to make GM and the other automotive giants tremble. He accused them of deliberately neglecting the safety of the American public. He accused them of propagating misinformation, or suppressing information when their cars were found to be defective. He accused them of putting profits before lives. He accused not only GM, but Ford, Chrysler, and American Motors. They were guilty of valuing style over safety and neglecting to use technology already available to solve safety problems.

Ralph estimated that nearly every year there were losses totaling $9 billion in property damage, medical expenses, insurance overhead and other expenses connected with highway accidents. He started his book this way: "For over half a century the automobile has brought death, injury, and the most inescapable sorrow and deprivation to millions of people."

Ralph was acutely aware that design is a major factor in automobile safety, and that the technical means for making cars safe are available. He found a man named Hugh de Haven who had crashed in a collision of two light aircraft and survived because his cockpit remained intact. De Haven had spent the next few decades, often at great risk to himself, attempting to apply the principles of safe cockpits to cars, and he had been laughed at for his trouble. But he proved that safer cars could be made, that impact-resisting bumpers, effective up to 20 miles per hour without damage to car or individual, could easily be designed and installed.

Another man, James Ryan, a professor, researched and designed devices to reduce the impact of crashes, confident that the job could be done. Ryan did improve on the bumper idea, frequently testing his own devices by strapping himself into a special cabin and driving into a wall.

"On November 13, 1957," Ralph related in his book, "accompanied by a graduate student, Ryan got into a 1956 Ford car, fitted with this bumper, at Holloman Air Force Base in New Mexico. The car was driven into a solid crash barricade at twenty miles per hour, with no injuries resulting to the passengers or the vehicle."

Drunken drivers are a menace to motorists, as automobile manufacturers like to point out. But badly designed cars are as great a menace. After doing some poking around on his own, Ralph made a list of some of the most dangerous parts of cars.

In the California crash involving the blue Corvair, the steering wheel had killed the driver. Originally, steering wheels were flat and set on a stiff column. Then the industry tried a depressed steering wheel, with the hub of the standard column below the rim of the wheel, or indented. However, what was really needed was an energy-absorbing steering wheel with a different mount. In the demolished Corvair, the front wheel had been displaced, driving the column through the chest of the driver. The angle of the axle was also at fault in that accident.

Ralph cites the testimony of Dr. Horace Campbell, a Denver surgeon, who was asked to look at a car in which a man had died solely of a broken neck. " 'His car, a 1961 Corvair, was extensively damaged at the left front corner. The hub of the steering wheel was displaced, by actual measurement against another car of the same make, two feet upward and backward. It broke his neck. He had no other injuries of consequence. The man who towed his car in told me that in every car of this make which he brought in with the left front deformation, the steering shaft is driven backward, often more than a foot!' "

Another investigator, Murray Burnstine, said of the stylistic changes in the steering wheels, "In many cases, they function only well enough to allow the motorist to die in the hospital instead of on the road."

Another cause of injuries for motorists is the instrument panel. For a while it was fashionable to make car instrument panels look like those of jet fighters. Knobs, chrome, and pushbuttons are glamorous but also confusing and, ultimately, dangerous when the driver has to look away from the road to find his lights or close an electric window. Ralph pointed out that even if dashboards were padded, the knobs presented a threat, and he cited the case of a little girl who had lost an eye because of a knob. Also, since the dashboard was the same distance from the front seat passenger, with no steering column to run into, he could fracture his skull as easily on the panel as he could by going through the windshield.

De Haven's studies showed that a body can stand considerable impact if the impact is spread over an area. He cited the example the old medieval shields, which spread the impact of an attacking blade, while the blade itself is a point of concentrated impact. Sharp projections above dashboards and knobs, not to mention mirrors, are points of concentrated impact. One doctor spoke of a woman who had nearly her whole scalp torn off by a badly placed screw in a bracket. It was obviously part of the design, he said, "not with injury production in mind, but nevertheless its placement there undoubtedly in this case, as in probably many others, resulted in unnecessary injury."

Windshields can also be dangerous, Ralph found. Too hard a glass can kill when a head smashes against it. If it is too soft, the passenger goes through, possibly with sharp glass edges severing his head from his body or slicing open his arteries.

"In order to minimize injury," Ralph pointed out, "a windshield that is struck by a vehicle occupant must have two important qualities: it must not be so hard that the head snaps back with a concussion or fracture, nor must it yield easily so that the blow breaks it with resultant hideous lacerations."

And to keep from going into the windshield, a rider needs a seat belt. Ralph pointed out that safety belts have been in existence since the pre-World War I planes, when half the battle of flying was to keep from being sucked from one's cockpit by the wind. Then the seat belt idea was transferred to commercial aircraft, but its application to automobiles "lagged greatly then, as it has ever since."

The problem has always been getting people to wear safety belts. When they were first tried, the industry dropped the feature because no one was interested in using them. When they were offered as an "extra," even fewer people bought them. Finally a campaign was begun, and today more people are wearing belts, but many wear them only on superhighways, and it is a fact that most accidents occur on short trips.

However, seat belts alone are not enough. It has been found that shoulder harnesses are better. Of course, unless they are of good quality and properly installed, even shoulder harnesses can be a hazard. And often belts are badly installed.

Ralph found even more basic, though subtler, dangers. The new "P-N-R-D-L" indicators on automatic transmissions were confusing. People had to look to see what gear they were in and frequently confused R or reverse with L or D, the forward gears. After several years of frustration, the automotive giants finally, and reluctantly, changed the gear indicator to "P-R-N-D-L," thus eliminating the possibility of a driver's going forward when he wanted to go backward. But it was an uphill struggle. A solution may seem obvious and simple, but, as Ralph discovered, nothing is obvious when you are dealing with corporate giants.

There is the problem of ethics, for example, if you are an engineer. The code of ethics of the National Society of Engineers reads in part, "The Engineer will have proper regard for the safety, health and welfare of the public in the performance of his professional duties. If his engineering judgment is overruled by nontechnical authority, he will clearly point out the consequences. He will notify the proper authority of any observed conditions which endanger public safety and health. . . . He will not complete, sign or seal plans and/or specifications that are not of a design safe to the public health and welfare. . . . If the client or employer insists on such unprofessional conduct, he shall notify the proper authorities and withdraw from further service on the project."

But the acceptance of engineering as a profession (like law and medicine) is slow, and there is less cohesiveness among engineers than there is among doctors, yet both deal with human life.

Such professionalism is perfectly possible, Ralph discovered. "The creative work published on the theoretical aspects of automotive technology from tires to engines to vehicle dynamics . . . has for years been far greater at European universities and technical institutes than that coming from American academic institutions or the American automobile industry. The European research has long been the vanguard of the automotive engineering discipline."

European manufacturers found that disc brakes were safer than regular brakes. They were available in Europe for ten years before an American manufacturer offered them, and then it was as an expensive option for two wheels only.

Perhaps the most telling demonstration of the industry's resistance to using available technology was the proud demonstration (after all of Ryan's conclusive work) in 1972 by a major automobile manufacturer of a "safety" bumper that did not collapse on impact—up to five miles an hour! After that, it went *crunch* like any other.

States have instituted complicated licensing procedures to ensure as far as possible that drivers are at least minimally competent, but standards of automobile inspection are by no means so stringent. Courts generally assume that if a driver has had an accident, he has broken the law or behaved negligently; they do not, as a matter of course, raise the possibility that the accident was caused by mechanical failure. The American Automobile Association has long been concerned for motorists' welfare, supplying them with maps, road services, and lobbies to fight tolls and taxes. But, critics say, it has hesitated to rock the boat about safety problems despite pressure brought to bear on it from knowledgeable younger factions whose bible is *Unsafe at Any Speed.*

Even motor magazines have been guilty of neglecting safety issues. When the Corvair came out, many of these magazines urged drivers to improve their skills in order to meet the challenge of this temperamental car. Since the magazines depend on industry advertising, they could not risk saying that the Corvair was just plain dangerous to drive.

The 1966 Auto Safety Act was a major victory whose impact can be seen in every vehicle on the road. Collapsible steering columns and stronger bumpers are standard on many models, and seatbelts are virtually mandatory. The Act made the industry switch its advertising emphasis from "horsepower" to "safety." Safety research was begun in a desultory way by manufacturers. And the recall system was begun. There have been improvements, but not enough of them—and certainly not soon enough for hundreds of thousands of people involved in collisions since 1966.

Since 1966 the number of annual highway deaths has not decreased, and in some areas it has increased.

In spite of the Act, neither the cars nor driver and passenger safety has improved enough to make an impact on the death toll. It is true that just recently a slight dip in the annual auto death toll was announced by the National Safety Council, and some observers attributed it directly to Ralph Nader's efforts. There are, after all, now seat and shoulder harnesses, better padded dashboards, and safer steering wheels. There are side beams on many models, and other protective features. But it is impossible to say for sure that Ralph's efforts have been the cause for the reversed trend, and even if it could be proved, he himself would say the reversal is only a drop in the bucket.

For planned obsolescence still renders cars highly dangerous after a specified amount of miles when a universal joint, a bearing, or even an axle may give way.

In the first four months of 1972 over 7 million cars were recalled—more than were sold—and on top of that, some of the recalls had to be recalled!

Recalls are now so commonplace as to risk being ignored. Owners often regard the soft wording of the manufacturers' letters as an indication that the changes and repairs are not essential. Fortunately, however, more and more are wising up to the message behind the courteous letter: if the car is not fixed, the owner risks death. Owners grumble, shrug, and accept the recalls as evidence of the shoddy way American corporations are run.

It seems that some Americans do not really care.

They spend more on cigarettes and liquor than on automotive safety. They do not fasten seat belts that might save their lives if they careen into a tree, or shoulder harnesses that might protect them from a fractured skull or a broken neck.

Research with air bags and impact tests has proved that well-designed dashboards can make cars safer. With proper padding to spread the impact and resilient metal underneath the padding, according to John Swearington, one of the researchers, "We should be able to eliminate hundreds of thousands of facial injuries. With proper design, a person could hit his head on a panel at forty feet per second with no injuries at all, while presently people are dying from impacts at fifteen feet per second."

The 1966 Auto Safety Act has not been a total loss. Besides the improvements mentioned, it also paved the way for other consumer protection acts. It broke through the barrier of the seemingly impermeable auto corporation lobby.

Yet Ralph Nader's indictment holds: "When and if the automobile is designed to free millions of human beings from unnecessary mutilation, these men (those people who have conformed to corporate ritual), like their counterparts in universities and government who knew of the holdup on safer automobile engineering and yet remained silent year after year, will look back with shame on the time when common candor was considered courage."

CHAPTER

6

Meet the Petersons, an average American family whose diet, like that of most American families, consists of breakfast, lunch, dinner, and snacks. Like most Americans, the Petersons believe that they live healthy lives and eat nutritious food. But let's look a little closer.

It is Sunday, and the Peterson family sits down to an old-fashioned Sunday dinner—or so they think. There is soup to begin with, followed by turkey, tomato salad, fresh green beans, and strawberry shortcake for dessert. It all tastes very good, and from the satisfied look on Mrs. Peterson's face, you can tell that she has done well by her family.

Or has she?

Timmy Peterson is only four. He loves two things above all others: one is packaged fruit-flavor drink mix, right out of the envelope. The other is hot dogs. Timmy can go through more hot dogs for his size than you would imagine. His father says he stuffs them into a hollow leg. Mrs. Peterson indulges Timmy's passion for drink mix, and hot dogs are a convenient lunch. After all, he and the rest of the family eat a hearty breakfast of concentrated orange juice, cereal, toast, and coffee (or milk). And at night they have their main meal.

Jennifer is eight. She goes to school, and her mother packs a lunch for her every day. With two children, it takes a lot of time to prepare food, and Mrs. Peterson likes the "convenience" foods processed especially for lunch boxes. She often gives Jennifer bologna sandwiches, because Jennifer especially likes them, and canned puddings which thaw from the freezer in time for lunch.

Mr. Peterson is a salesman, always on the go. For lunch he usually grabs a hamburger and a chocolate bar for quick energy. He knows he'll have a hearty meal in the evening.

The Petersons have the eating habits of most families. They like snack foods, cola drinks and chips, and they can afford the quickly prepared items that let Mrs. Peterson get out of the kitchen. They live under the impression that they, like most American families, are among the lucky people in the world who are adequately nourished and receive proper amounts of vitamins, minerals, carbohydrates, proteins, and other essential items every day.

They are wrong. The Petersons, like many middle-class families, are inadequately nourished. They think they are eating well because their stomachs are full and their tastebuds are satisfied. So are their eyes: the packaging of many foods is so attractive that they must—the reasoning goes—be good for you.

Let's look (as Ralph Nader did) at the food the Petersons are eating. More than likely, for starters, their orange juice is watered down. Orange juice sold as such need only be 50 percent juice. The other 50 percent can be anything, including flavored water. An "ade" (orangeade, lemonade) need only be 25 percent juice, and a "drink" (orange drink, pop) is required by Federal standards to have only 10 percent juice in it, which really is like drinking flavored water. Chances are that the Petersons' juice is watered only 10 percent. Manufacturers cannot get away with more than that because customers could detect thinness and would turn to a product made by another manufacturer.

What about the toast for breakfast? If it was what usually passes for bread, a spongy, tasteless product, it probably was made from flour that had been so processed as to lose all of its nutritive value (ground, bleached, and preserved), powdered eggs (if any), an emulsifier, synthetic vitamins to make up for lost value, and artificial flavoring. Recently, one of the major bakers of this type of bread came under attack from the government because the company's advertising gives the impression that the bread has tremendous nutritive value. Many people grow up knowing only that kind of bread. If Mrs. Peterson had ever tasted homemade bread, she would probably be horrified at the difference in taste but go right on buying commercial bread because she is under the impression that making bread at home with unbleached flour is a time-consuming and difficult process (it isn't).

Cereals have come under the same kind of attack, on nutritional grounds. It has long been known that vegetable protein is inferior to animal protein, and cereals are high in calories for the amount of protein they provide.

Timmy's favorite lunch is more than likely 33 percent fat. Unless the package states otherwise (and sometimes even when it does), the "franks" contain beef, pork, veal, and many leftovers which have been processed, treated with chemicals such as monosodium glutamate (MSG), a chemical suspected to be a health hazard, saccharin (also suspect), meat tenderizer and many other things, including food coloring.

Until cyclamates were banned, Timmy's envelope of drink mix could have contained two and a half times as much cyclamate as has been estimated could be harmful to him. (Cyclamates in large quantities cause bladder cancer in rats.)

Mr. Peterson's hamburger and Jennifer's bologna are also high in fats, not to mention meat tenderizer, food coloring, artificial flavoring, MSG, and other substances. Mr. Peterson's chocolate bar more than likely has cellulose fiber filler in it.

The Petersons' Sunday dinner contains: artificial flavoring and MSG in the soup, air and added oils in the turkey (which was fed antibiotics to help it grow fatter more quickly as well as to ward off disease), tomatoes that have been injected with gas and coated with wax to make them look more attractive, beans sprayed with several kinds of long-lasting pesticides, strawberries which have also been sprayed, and commercial short-cake made from the same unnutritious ingredients as the artificial breakfast bread: powdered eggs, bleached flour, artificial flavoring, preservatives and emulsifiers.

The worst of it is that Mrs. Peterson doesn't know that her family is undernourished. Many of the ingredients used in the foods her family eats are not on the label—such as the caffeine, a mildly addictive stimulant, in Jennifer's cola drink.

Ralph Nader is acutely aware of the problems involved in the food industry. He will not eat any prepared foods. He is suspicious of ground meat and prepared meats. He is acutely aware of anything that will harm human beings internally or externally. Coming as he does from a family that has been associated with food for most of its life, Ralph is something of an expert on how food should be prepared in restaurants. He despises eating in food establishments, and regards every mouthful with suspicion. "You never know," he says, "what goes into what you eat in a restaurant, whether mice are nesting under the flour, or roaches in the crackers." One of the first projects he instigated after the Auto Safety Act was the meat bill.

Because food is essential to life, the food industry is a multi *billion*-dollar business. In an effort to stimulate more buying, food processors have come up with imaginative new products that have contributed in increasing amounts to the image of Americans as overfed and undernourished.

Meat—animal protein—has been emphasized since the early part of the century as essential to good health. Many Americans consume more meat in a month than many people in so-called "underdeveloped" countries eat in a year—or even in two years. Americans have almost a fetish about meat, and they buy it in great quantities.

Early in this century, Upton Sinclair wrote a book called *The Jungle,* a horrific novel telling of unspeakable conditions in meat-packing plants: filthy equipment, meat stored on dirty floors, diseased carcasses being ground up and used in sausage along with spittle, rodent excreta, rodent corpses and flies—all to be sold in the friendly neighborhood grocery to unsuspecting customers. Ralph found similar conditions when he began investigating meat-packing plants that did not ship their products across state lines and thus were not regulated by Federal law.

Only one giant firm had all its plants under Federal inspection; the others had plants that prepared and processed meats to be sold only within the state where they were located, in order to take advantage of weaker state laws and enforcement. Although many of the giants were phasing out their small plants because they found them to be too costly, in 1972 there were still a number in operation which had not hired enough federal inspectors or veterinarians to inspect animals, and had not renovated rundown, rat-infested plants. While none of these plants was sufficiently filthy to be closed down, all presented health dangers.

Around the time Ralph started talking to the Senate Agriculture Committee, a journalist named Nathan Kotz acquired some "private" files that in official language read like a 1967 version of *The Jungle*. In a Pulitzer Prize-winning article, he published the findings of these reports. Spurred to action by that journalistic scoop, pursued by the hound of consumer affairs Ralph Nader, and embarrassed by a solicitation made by the agriculture lobby, Congress passed the Wholesome Meat Act. Much of its text had been suggested by Ralph.

While the bill was being debated, Ralph focused publicity on it by asking Betty Furness, then in charge of the government's Department of Consumer Affairs, what she thought of it. She refused to comment and later came out in favor of a government-supported bill that was not as strong as the Wholesome Meat Act proposed by Congressman Neil Smith of Iowa, who had been trying to get the Federal meat regulations changed for five years.

Finally the Mondale-Montoya bill was passed and signed by President Lyndon Johnson. It was a compromise bill that gave states two years to upgrade intrastate packing plants. If they did not make the deadline, the federal government could take over the job of supervision. This gave states the choice of losing their "states' rights" by having the federal government run their meat industries, or upgrading them at considerable expense.

Another food crisis came when problems in the poultry industry were exposed. For many years a virus that caused cancer in chickens had been spreading, and yet the infected chickens had been still going to market. When that fact was revealed, people were outraged. While there was not then any evidence that cancer in chickens causes cancer in humans, Ralph pointed out that "There also isn't any proof to show the disease can't be transmitted. And the research on this has been very recent and not thorough at all . . . the inspection teams can study only a small percentage of the poultry going onto the market. Since nearly every bird has avian leukosis [the technical name for the virus-caused cancer] to some degree, that means a lot of bad poultry is probably slipping onto your dinner table."

Debate over these revelations resulted in the Wholesome Poultry Act of 1968, a bill similar to the Wholesome Meat Act. Chickens showing tumors disappeared from the market.

But the passage of the bills was not in itself a cure. Although they now exist on the books, they have been ineffectual, as have some of the other bills Ralph stimulated. That is not because the bills are badly written but because the Federal government has neither money nor manpower to enforce them.

Ralph is the first person to admit the failure of the acts of which he has been co-author. "It's not in the bills themselves," he says, "but in the powerlessness of consumers to force the government to implement the bills. Until we can compel the government to enforce the bills which Congress has passed, we will continue to be defrauded in the industries which touch the most personal aspects of our lives."

The meat and poultry problems are relatively simple compared with the problems of controlling the substances that are added to our foods.

More than 278 substances are added to our foods that are on the Federal Food and Drug Administration list of additives "generally recognized as safe." These are all substances that have been used since before 1958. Any new substance has to pass federal testing and approval. But some items have been on this list that were subsequently removed. Cyclamate sweeteners were attacked on the basis that they caused bladder cancer in rats, and they were removed from the list. Saccharin, a sweetener in use for several decades, has been removed from the list for a similar reason.

Hundreds of other additives are not subject to these regulations and are not on this list. They are natural flavors and oils. Many items must be mentioned on the labels of the products in which they are used, but the law is very hazy in some cases. For example, the bottle of cola that one of the Peterson kids might have when coming home from school probably has caffeine in it, although it doesn't say so on the label. Several years ago the cola drink makers convinced the powers that be that caffeine was essential to the manufacture of their product. "Essential" ingredients are not required by law to be listed on labels, although many manufacturers of food products do list them. Caffeine is a mildly habit-forming stimulant that many parents do not want their children to drink. Many people with metabolism problems and some other health problems cannot have caffeine in their diets.

The Food and Drug Administration ruled that cola drinks did not have to have caffeine listed as a substance or ingredient on their labels, although other drinks did, because the cola companies insisted that the use of caffeine in their products was common knowledge.

It takes nearly $100,000 to put a new additive through the test standards of the FDA. But new additives appear every year. What are their purposes? They preserve some foods, such as bread, from going stale. They are components in artificial flavorings. They make whipped topping foam. They flavor.

Additives can also deceive. There are additives that can make old meat look fresh. There are additives that can change flavors. It is an old joke in the ice cream industry that before more rigid regulations were imposed the "leftovers" from batches of other flavors of ice cream were thrown together into the batch of chocolate because the latter, in combination with additives, disguised the combined flavors of the others.

Caffeine in a heart patient's diet is only one example of the dangers of additives. Some countries (not the United States) have banned monosodium glutamate, a flavor-enhancer used in most prepared foods and most heavily in oriental foods. Some people who eat a lot of MSG have strange symptoms, known as the "Chinese restaurant syndrome," although MSG is used in most restaurants. These people experience stiff necks, tingling down their spines, and sometimes headaches, dizziness, and nausea.

In a recent article in *Scientific American*, G. O. Kermode said, "One cannot be fully sure of the safety of an additive until it has been consumed by people of all ages in specified amounts over a long period of time and has been shown conclusively by careful toxicological examination to have no harmful effects." Even if this sort of testing were possible, it remains that "Many additives by nature are of extremely low potential toxicity. It is therefore difficult to determine their possible hazards to man, even after exhaustive testing. It is probably true to say that there will always be an area of doubt concerning the possible effects of ingesting small amounts of additives over the course of a lifetime."

Ralph sums it up this way. "Meeting these taste tests does not lead, unfortunately, to fulfilling the requisites of purity, wholesomeness, safety, and nutrition. In fact, very often the degradation of these standards proceeds from the cosmetic treatment of food or is its direct cost by-product. For example, the nutritional deception about 'enriched white flour' covers up the permanent stripping in the processing stages of most nutrients. Coloring additives, preservatives, seasonings, and tenderizers camouflage the rapid increase of fat content in frankfurters (33 percent of weight on the average in 1969), their decrease in meat protein, and the substandard quality of the meat. The hazards of hundreds of untested or inadequately tested food additives are about to be given some of the governmental attention that they have so long deserved.

"Further, the heavy promotional emphasis on 'unfoods' such as near-zero nutrition 'snacks,' chemically doused bakery goods, and soft drinks have a serious distorting effect on young people's food habits and concepts of nutrition. Millions are growing up watching the television ads and believing their messages that Pepsi-Cola and Coca-Cola provide health and vigor. Small wonder then that the United States Department of Agriculture shows a decline in nutritional adequacy of American family diets."

To top it all off, we are not, as we often want to believe, the healthiest nation in the world. Life expectancy in the United States has not increased. Infant mortality has not declined, and the average American family, which has more than enough to eat, is not getting enough nutrients.

When Ralph's raiders' report *The Chemical Feast* was published, it created quite a stir. The prime target of its salvo was the Food and Drug Administration; the secondary target was the growth of monopolies in the food industry.

The Food and Drug Administration is charged with the responsibility for guarding the nation's health by regulating what chemicals and drugs are "safe" for people to use. Oddly enough, this vital agency is grossly underfinanced and understaffed. Most surprising of all, it has no enforcement authority. It cannot go out and arrest someone for breaking the food and drug laws. It can file suit, but this is often an extremely time-consuming process.

The Nader report brought to light that the FDA was misusing funds by going after "quacks" rather than the large corporate manufacturers of drugs and users of additives. It used every spy tool known to modern electronics to put sellers who mislabeled vitamins and health foods in jail, while it ignored warnings on cyclamates and saccharin, failed to question the iron content in bread that can cause malignant and fatal blood disease in men, or the fact that in eighteen years the United States has risen from fifth place to thirteenth in infant mortality figures.

The FDA spent thirteen years putting a noted psychoanalyst named Wilhelm Reich in jail for selling products known as orgone boxes without FDA clearance. The orgone boxes were supposed to improve health and promote longevity. That Reich was breaking the law is a fact. But the FDA spent thirteen years investigating, tailing, and harassing him and came up with some wholly unjust accusations. FDA reported that he had no medical degree (he did, in fact, have an M.D. from the prestigious University of Vienna and was one of Sigmund Freud's original students). It accused him of living with a woman (he did indeed: his wife). Though it had nothing to do with Reich's research (he claimed to have found a cure for cancer), the FDA inspector carried out orders obtained by the FDA in court to destroy some of his pamphlets, including Reich's analytic classic, *Character Analysis*, which had been hailed as one of the major breakthroughs in psychoanalysis. The FDA inspector actually burned the books. Reich observed sadly that he had left Nazi Germany because his books had been burned and never expected to see it happen in the United States.

Reich was sent to the Lewisburg Penitentiary, where he died within seventeen months. After his death, the FDA spent a lot of time and money trying to find more of his pamphlets and material. The Nader report says, "It is an irony that in the case of Wilheim Reich much of the work that the FDA wished to suppress was highly thought of by members of the psychoanalytic profession, and that the FDA knew this to be the case before the prosecution of Reich was launched. The State Department document filed four years before the action has said, "It is of interest that all but one of the psychiatrists [in Norway] consulted for information about Dr. Reich spoke of his psychiatric work with the greatest respect while without exception denying the validity of his biological work."

For thirteen years the FDA harassed Dr. Reich. No one denies that he broke the law by selling his "orgone" devices. But for nineteen years the FDA ignored mounting evidence against cyclamates until, when they were banned in 1969, the food industry had more than a billion dollars tied up in cyclamate-sweetened foods.

The FDA, Ralph asserted, seems more concerned with the number of violators it can bring to court than with the size or extent of the violations. Thus the small violators are pursued and harassed while the large corporations continue to market products that are potentially hazardous to human beings.

Of the 2,500 substances that are being added to foods, only about half have been throughly investigated by the FDA. The Nader report makes short work of the

FDA's scientific and management capabilities. It cites scores of studies that have found the FDA to be inefficient. The agency lives in constant terror of having its miniscule budget cut by an irate congressman whose corporate constituent has had his toes stepped on by the FDA and may be a big contributor to his election campaigns.

The FDA needs many things, Ralph has declared. It needs an efficient way of operating. It needs an adequate scientific research staff. It needs an adequate appropriation that is not tied to the purse-strings of major campaign contributors, which include some of the food giants. It needs enforcement powers so that its actions are not tied to local (and locally financed) courts. It needs to turn its guns away from the occasional quack and aim them at the giant corporations who are adulterating our food and slowly gaining a monopoly over food production and preparation in the United States.

As for additives, a commission of the World Health Organization has set standards for them. "The first is that the use of an additive is justified only when it has the purpose of maintaining a food's nutritional quality, enhancing its keeping quality or stability, making the food attractive, providing aid in processing, packing, transporting, or storing food or providing essential components for foods for special diets; and then an additive is not justified if the proposed level of use constitutes a hazard to the consumer's health, if the additive causes a substantial reduction in the nutritive value of the food, if it disguises faulty quality or the use of processing and handling techniques that are not al-

86

lowed, if it deceives the customer or if the desired effect can be obtained by other manufacturing processes that are economically and technologically satisfactory."

The problem of monopoly falls under the jurisdiction of the Department of Justice, but the FDA is constantly involved in investigating food manufacturing processes that have grown out of monopolistic situations. Ninety-five percent of all the soup that is sold as of 1969 was produced by the Campbell's Soup Company. More than half of American cheese is sold by Borden and Kraft. Kraft (National Dairy) and Corn Products sell most of the salad dressing on the market. These industries exercise a powerful lobby in Washington known as the "Food Group." They have become conglomerates and in some cases have been bought by conglomerates, and are part of the movement toward fewer corporations holding greater economic (and therefore political) power in the United States.

Perhaps most of all we (and the FDA) need to change our attitudes about chemicals in our foods. Instead of "maximum safe levels" there should be no levels at all allowed until the chemical has been established to be "safe" or generally useful to human welfare.

Perhaps the Petersons, fond as they are of their favorite foods, whould have fewer colds, better general health and less chance of genetic damage if they read a few labels and investigated the nature of their Sunday dinner, which may indeed be, in Ralph Nader's words, a "chemical feast."

CHAPTER

7

With his concern about the human body and everything that directly affects it, Ralph Nader is life-oriented. He cares not just about statistics but about the lives they represent, not just about the quantity of facts but about the quality of life behind them.

His personal involvement in improving the quality of our lives led inadvertently to two tragedies. One concerned his endorsement of Jock Yablonski as candidate for president of the United Mine Workers, the other an investigation into the operation of nursing homes.

Down in the barren valleys of West Virginia and Pennsylvania, coal mining is still a major industry. Strip mining is not the only method. Men still go thousands of feet down in the mines to sweat the coal out of the seams. They brave the dangers of cave-ins and collapse.

Daily they face the possibility of gas explosions and fires. According to labor statistics, coal mining is the most hazardous work of all.

Supposedly mine safety had advanced by the time Ralph came on the scene. But he was concerned with a more insidious enemy than the gas explosions and terrible fires that claimed hundreds of lives in the mines every year.

Its name was black lung disease.

Ralph found that one out of every two miners suffers from it; only one in every thirty people working in the mines is likely to suffer some other sort of injury in a year.

Black lung disease is a horrible illness. Inhaled coal dust particles are deposited in the sensitive tissues, and in addition miners breathe in the carbon dioxide that collects in the shafts. In the mines this is known as blackdamp or chokedamp. The gas combines with the natural body fluids and, among other things, forms acids that combine to increase the erosion to lungs. Small air spaces or aveoli in the lungs become distended. Gradually they stiffen, as in the case of emphysema. Breathing becomes labored. Often lung cancers develop. All the associated complications are lumped under the name black lung disease.

The miners had a second problem. Their union was one of the richest and most powerful unions in the country. John L. Lewis had fought his way to leadership in an era that saw machine gunnings and bombings as the leadership fought to sort itself out and struggled against low wages, dangerous working conditions, and pitiable living conditions above ground.

John L. Lewis won many battles for the miners, but his involvement with union politics—especially the AFL-CIO—led him further and further away from immediate problems, although he never lost his personal identification with the miners, or they with him.

In 1969, when Lewis was a craggy 89 years old, the leadership of the United Mine Workers was open. Everyone thought that Tony Boyle, who said he was Lewis' political heir, could not be defeated. He controlled the presses, the money, and the politicians in the union. There were a lot of people who hated him and would have liked to get rid of him. Their complaint was that the powerful union leadership was far removed from the people it was supposed to be working for. It worked to increase its wealth and political muscle, and it worked especially to increase the salaries and profits of its officers.

Ralph's concern for the miners was very real, and he felt that the only way the corrupt workings of the unions could be exposed was to find someone to run for president against Boyle.

He finally convinced Jock Yablonski to run. Yablonski had been a loyal member of Boyle's regime. But he had taken the measure of his union. He had supported wildcat strikes which were not supported by the union management, and had condemned laws and finally the union itself for insensitivity to the miners' suffering. He told Ralph that if he ran against Boyle he would be killed. Ralph urged him to take the chance. The Kennedy and King assassinations were fresh in everyone's mind but Ralph believed Yablonski would be too much in the public eye for assassins to risk killing him. Ralph then began to arrange for Yablonski's candidacy. He wrote the statement Yablonski made on entering the race, and he worked for Yablonski to get proper press coverage. He arranged for a law student to be with Yablonski throughout the campaign, which was bitter and violent.

Ralph was venturing into something dangerously close to politics, and he knew it. Even though he made the behind-the-scenes arrangements, he stayed fairly aloof from the proceedings. But he was personally present—a highly unusual circumstance—the night Yablonski made his announcement in a heavily guarded hall.

The stakes were very high. "You can't just let these miners go on dying," he said. "They should receive workmen's compensation, like every other worker who's injured or disabled on the job. And you can believe that half of the miners will be."

Ralph was also upset about safety. "You can almost smell death," he said of the mist-shrouded valleys of Appalachia. "Those men—and their families—never know when the men go down in the mines if they'll ever come out again. These people are suffering, and no one who can do something about it cares—the mine owners, the state governments, or even the miners' own union."

Ralph tended to disappear as the campaign progressed, not because he was copping out, but because he had never promised to do more than help with the publicity and act as adviser. He also met with some of Boyle's people and quickly realized that the whole campaign tactic was going to be for each man to smear the other's character and accomplishments.

But what was most surprising and grim was that as the inmost scandals of the UMW were revealed and hurled like rocks at each other by Boyle and Yablonski, no one followed them up. There were accusations of fixed elections, strongarm tactics, misuse of funds and more. The Labor Department did nothing. The FBI did nothing. Apparently no one did care about the miners, and American citizens were quite content to let them solve their own problems by whatever methods they chose.

Yablonski, during the campaign, was maligned, mauled, and beaten. And he lost, in some places by huge margins. The 1969 election was a disaster, not only because of the generally sordid nature of the campaign and the violence, but because after the election, in January of 1970, Yablonski, his wife, and his 25-year-old daughter were brutally murdered in their beds by thugs who broke into the house and shot them. They were shot because they knew too much and because after his defeat it was suspected that Yablonski might go to the authorities with proof of some of the scandals that had been aired during the election.

It took that murder to get the Labor Department into action. It spent $500,000 to conduct an investigation into the Yablonski murders, the election, and the UMW. It finally came to the conclusion that there was not enough evidence to connect the violence of the campaign with the murder of Yablonski and his wife and daughter.

In 1972, however, the whole issue was reopened. The alleged Yablonski murderers were found out and tried. The labor department reopened its investigations of the union and especially of Tony Boyle. But although the UMW had come before the public eye, it had not been cowed or changed.

When Ralph heard the news of the Yablonski murders he was stunned. "I can't believe it," he kept saying. He had failed to recognize the ruthlessness of the men involved in the UMW setup and he had miscalculated their capacity for getting what they wanted at any cost. He had gradually become disillusioned with the ability of laws to be effective without enforcement, but he had not realized that the strongarm tactics of the 1930s were still operative.

In 1970 Ralph was again involved with death, but it was an investigation that exposed concealed violence to human dignity. The miners' violence was open, and even Yablonski had an inkling of what was to come. But for the many helpless invalids consigned to nursing homes by their trusting families, as well as by families who no longer cared, the quality of life was unbearable.

Imagine a large, white clapboard mansion that has been converted into a nursing home, or even one of the newer concrete-and-glass varieties. Inside are old people. Some have come to convalesce and will leave. But for most, it is the end of the line, and they are merely waiting to die.

In one room, a woman suffering from the aftermath

of a stroke is soaked in her own urine. No one has paid any attention to her since early morning, and it is doubtful that she will receive any until evening. In another room, an old man has fallen out of bed. Too feeble to call for help or move himself, he must wait on the cold floor until someone finds him. Theoretically there is a doctor on duty, but several weeks ago when someone died, no one could find a doctor to sign the death certificate.

The "nurse" on duty must take care of forty patients all by herself. She is not a registered nurse but a licensed practical nurse. She is not allowed to administer medications as a registered nurse can, although she is supposed to see that the patients receive theirs. Technically she cannot dispense drugs, but she has been known to give restless or disoriented patients—or patients she finds irritating—heavy doses of tranquilizers to lessen her work load.

Since visitors are few and rarely come except on weekends, she can pretty much let things ride during the day, as her relief does at night. It's a waiting house in any case, waiting for new ones to come and old ones to die. One old man in a nursing home tried to commit suicide but failed. He was labeled as having had a "relapse" and was carted off to a local hospital where there was little chance of his recovering.

Patients who are aware of what is going on retreat into themselves; their eyes show that they are living through their memories in another time, another place —anything to ignore and avoid the squalor of their surroundings: the smells, the cries, the surly care. One

94

old lady puts it this way: "They put dogs out of their misery to be humane. Why can't they treat us at least as well?"

The scandal of the nursing homes was brought to light by six girls, including a teacher, from the fashionable Miss Porter's, a girls' college preparatory school. One of the more exclusive schools of its kind, Miss Porter's has joined the social-awareness movement along with Madeira, St. Timothy's, Shipley, Westover, and Concord, to mention a few. Far from being naive, the girls who attend these schools are already acutely aware of some of the problems of society. Many of their parents are congressmen, senators, governors, ambassadors, corporate executives, or bankers. Although graduates of such schools traditionally become socialites, since 1959 an increasing number have entered public law, the Peace Corps, and other service professions.

Ralph Nader's name was already a household word by the time he suggested that the girls work for him as raiders in the nursing homes. He suspected not only that the patients were being mistreated, but also that the government was being cheated out of millions of dollars in Medicaid payments.

When he went to Miss Porter's to give his usual talk, the response was stronger than he had anticipated and many of the girls wanted to work as raiders. Ralph suggested the nursing home investigations as a summer project. The girls took jobs as nurses' aides for a few days or weeks, and then quit, refusing pay since they had stayed such a short time but taking with them their tales of horror. All of them testified before the Senate Committee on the Aging. Often their statements were heartrending. It became clear that too many people who have served their useful time in society are rewarded by serving time as inmates in establishments whose conditions resemble those of prisons. The majority of the elderly people in nursing homes were found to be living out their lives in "poverty, sickness, loneliness and powerlessness," along with the other elderly who were lucky enough—or perhaps not so lucky —to be on the "outside."

In the introduction to the report, Ralph said, "Neither full-fledged congressional hearings, nor the enforcement of adequate federal and state standards, nor the administrative inquiries and disclosures that are needed to reduce the institutional violence and cruelty that are rampant are available." He went on to describe "major fire disasters, fatal food contamination, corporate manipulations, drug experimentation beyond proper medical discretion, kickbacks in drug sales for residents, abysmal lack of medical supervision, and strong evidence that such abuses are more epidemic than episodic."

The report made some recommendations as to what should be done: enforcement of standards to be set up by the delinquent states, even if it means shutting down the homes, and even if the patients have nowhere else to go; publicly announced quality ratings; stricter medical supervision; training of aides; more legal restriction on home operators; community housing (to provide an alternative to nursing homes); stricter supervision and control of experimental drugs; social and psychiatric aid for the elderly, coupled with preventive medicine campaigns and a complete overhaul of the expensive, disorganized, inefficient and impersonal bureaucracy governing the affairs of the elderly.

What, then, do we mean by quality of life? There are several ways to look at it. It could mean the external circumstances under which people live. Or it could be looked at as the problem of the way people are allowed to die.

There is no question that the elderly in the United States depend on the government and on their families. There is also no question that both fail abysmally to help aging people lead dignified lives. For those older people who do not suffer from anything but advancing years, life often means being a "fifth wheel" in a young family's home. In an effort to "save Grandpa," grandpa is relieved of all work, especially manual labor, and the children are told to "leave him alone" because they annoy him. Grandpa begins to feel unwanted, useless, a burden to his children and their husbands or wives, and a drag on his grandchildren. No one wants him, listens to him or—except at mealtimes and specified hours of the day—cares for his mental needs.

One great old lady once said, "It's only my body that's old. Inside I'm still a little girl." This woman was nearing eighty, on crutches from arthritis in her hip. She cared for her husband, a marvelous old eccentric who loved to make money and continued to do so long after his retirement. He loved being babied and she indulged him, even to tying his shoes for him.

She lived for him, and for her 75 relatives, 15 charities and many young people whom she secretly helped. He lived for his art collection and the stock market. She followed a schedule that would leave many younger people exhausted. Both their minds were alert, clear, and totally aware of the changes going on in society and the world.

Needless to say, these old people were wealthy enough to want for nothing, and, indeed, secretly helped many of their elderly friends with donations that the bank would explain away with "You must have made an error in your calculations, sir." They never stopped learning, they never adopted society's attitude that they had to act "old," even when all their friends had died off, and they lived for their young friends.

But it does not take wealth to keep one's mental capabilities and healthy outlook on life. Many elderly people do live in dignity with their sons' or daughters' families. They are given responsibility in the household and are not ridiculed. Others live in poverty, yet retain personal pride.

But what about sick old people? What happens to them? What about their quality of life?

Recent studies show that many elderly people who are thought to have advanced "hardening of the arteries" which makes them "senile," or unable to think properly, really are retreating from reality—a cruel reality that tells them, truly or falsely, that whatever their former achievements may have been their lives are worth nothing. They feel that no one cares and that those they depend on wish they would go away and die quietly.

Such elderly people need both psychiatric and social help. It was once thought that if a person was beyond a certain age he was "too old" for psychiatric help, and that the short supply of doctors was better used on young people.

This attitude is simply part of the present American worship of youth. Advertising, films and other media fling it in the face of older people. Younger people condescend toward older citizens and are impatient with their hesitation and confusions.

And there are also the elderly people who are ill and dying and know it. What is the answer for them? It was once thought that the kindest thing to do was to put them in hospitals. But when hospitals become crowded, the dying are transferred to nursing "homes" that have proved to be little more than expensive jails or work-houses.

Many such places have the much-hailed intensive care units, where complex apparatus is used to keep patients alive, though "life" for them is closer to that of a vegetable than a human being. One woman put it this way: "I'd rather die poor and alone than be pushed, pulled, stuck, pumped, shocked, and monitored in one of those things." More and more people prefer to die "at home," no matter how sordid it might seem to out-siders.

The "Big Biology" to which Ralph Nader refers in every speech he makes has raised questions about many of these conditions and the attitudes that underlie them. It has always been a doctor's duty to preserve life as long as possible. But what if a patient's brain has stopped functioning? What if he is in intolerable, screaming pain? What if his disease has reduced him to such a pathetic state that he wishes to die in dignity without further surgery or treatment? Whose choice is the decision—the doctor's, the family's, or the person's who is suffering?

This is probably one of the hardest questions the human race has ever had to face. It falls into a new category of philosophy involved with medicine, psychiatry and religion. A new specialty has arisen in the medical profession: thanatology, or the problems of death.

Many doctors and nurses, oddly enough, are afraid of death, which may be one reason why nursing homes give such terrible care to terminal patients. The new study tries to overcome this weakness. Whereas death has rarely been discussed in the past, patients who know they are dying are now encouraged and helped from the first stage of disbelief, to the second stage of rage, the third stage of bargaining for time, the fourth stage of profound grief, and the final stage of acceptance and peace.

This new approach to death, coupled with a new approach to euthanasia, or merciful killing to put people out of their misery, has aroused howls of rage from certain groups. While "mercy-killing" is still illegal, some techniques aimed at relieving pain in terminal (doomed) cases fall short of the statutes about murder and manslaughter. For instance, (1) Administering a drug, such as a painkiller, to treat a variety of symptoms, but which may also have the indirect effect of killing the patient. This technique is known as the law of double effect. (2) Discontinuing the use of life-preserving gadgets. Taking a patient off a respirator, or the cardiographic machine, and pulling out the tubes carrying nutrition to or drainage from his body, allowing him to die naturally. Many old people hope they never see an intensive care unit. (3) Discontinuing treatment (such as chemical therapy, which often has terrible side-effects) except for relief of pain.

This new science, if that is what it is, is offensive to many people. First of all, who wants to think about death? Commercials convince you that some products will enable you to participate in the eternal volleyball game by the sea, never aging, never becoming ill.

Ralph Nader puts it this way, "If the Big Biology takes over, it may not let you die, even if you want to."

Big Biology is bigger than we know. It is now possible to take a frog's egg, put into its destroyed nucleus the nucleus of a cell from the frog's intestine, and grow an identical frog. If we were to do this with people, we would be artifically "creating" people or creating artificial "people"—we are not sure which. If a man needed a replacement kidney or heart, for example, there would be no need to search for a match. It would be there in the complete, humanlike "twin" that had grown from the cell of his own intestine.

What would be the status of such creatures? Would

they be human? Would they have rights? Would they be frozen for future use? What would be the psychological effect of having a laboratory-raised being who was biologically your own "twin"? The possibilities have not yet been explored fully even in science fiction.

CHAPTER
8

"Open your window and take a deep breath," says a recent ad, showing a pajama-clad individual leaning out of a city window. ". . . You'll feel lousy."

A *New Yorker* cartoon expressed the same condition without words. It showed a v-wedge of geese flying through the air, crying *"Honk, honk, honk, honk, honk, honk, honk, honk. . . ."* The second part of the cartoon showed them flying over a city through thick smog. *"Cough, cough, cough, cough, cough, cough, cough, cough. . . ."* and the third panel saw the geese flying once again in clean air, *"Honk, honk, honk, honk, honk, honk, honk, honk. . . ."*

But air pollution is no joke. Millions of tons of pollutants are poured into the air every year. Ralph Nader estimates that 60 percent of the pollutants are caused by cars. And the "tack-on" devices put on cars by manufacturers to help stop air pollution do not help very much.

Aside from the fact that it often smells bad and makes your nose itch and your eyes burn, why is air pollution so harmful? At the very least, it makes you feel sick. At the very worst, it can kill you.

Air pollution is responsible for thousands of deaths every year. People with respiratory diseases have trouble breathing during "inversions" in big cities, when a warm air mass is trapped under a cold air mass with no wind. Then the air becomes stale and pollutants build up. Sometimes the air is so bad that people begin to die.

There are other, less obvious effects of air pollution. Ralph Nader talked to scientists who have found that air pollutants given to rats and mice in proportionate quantities produce fewer, smaller, and more deformed young. It has long been known that smoking by pregnant women causes smaller babies. Ralph's raiders found that autopsies at the Philadelphia Zoo showed a sixfold increase in lung cancer in certain species of animals. Lead contaminates the air in such quantities that it kills especially susceptible zoo animals, such as the panther, or black leopard. One leopard in "clean air" Staten Island required two major hospitalizations because of lead poisoning in a one-year interval between 1970 and 1971.

It has also been found that smoking, admittedly bad for the smokers, is in some ways more harmful to nonsmokers who have to breathe in the gas and ashes from smokers' cigarettes.

It has been found that more than half of the population of cities where extensive construction is going on have asbestos in their lungs. Asbestos is so irritating to the body that people have been known to develop lung cancer around asbestos particles after a single, mild exposure such as cutting plasterboard for art projects or soundproofing. Yet on any breezy day in New York you can watch the asbestos drifting off construction sites and falling gently on the people.

Air is not the only carrier of pollution. Food and water are also prime carriers. The Hudson River is one of the filthiest waterways in the world, industry has killed off Lake Erie, and made the Cuyohoga River an official fire hazard in Ohio. That river has caught fire several times from combustible pollutants poured into its waters.

Pollution is more than the smell of a coffee plant nauseating Manhattan on a wrong evening breeze from New Jersey. Or beer cans on remote rocky outcroppings. Or even lung cancers and death. It is so widespread as to be almost inconceivable.

When Thor Heyerdahl crossed the Atlantic in Ra I and Ra II he found shocking evidence of pollution all the way across thousands of miles of ocean. Garbage, oil —all the wastes of human life. He found fewer forms of sea life and more evidence that man is rapidly destroying his planet. Man is even polluting space. Thousands of pieces of space junk are orbiting the earth, most of them headed for a fiery death after a few decades, but some in orbits that will keep them aloft for hundreds of years.

105

Several kinds of pollution are not detectable by man at all until he sees the monstrous results. Radiation is hard to detect. People cannot smell it, feel it, taste it, or sense it in any way. When radiation disease struck the people of Hiroshima and Nagasaki, man began to learn that the power of the atom was the power to kill with suffering beyond imagination. Yet radiation pollution comes from color TV sets, microwave ovens (in many homes, restaurants and aircraft), dental x-rays and doctors' x-rays, far in excess of the minimum "safe" dosages. To these are added doses from such enterprises as nuclear electric power plants—which raises a question: Is it better to die of lung cancer from air pollution caused by coal-burning power plants, or of that caused by excess radiation?

Several towns in uranium country have been built over radioactive salt mines. Landfill for some houses comes from radioactive waste piles.

Carbon monoxide is another secret killer. Coming from factories and especially from cars, it kills by suffocation, strangling red cells.

Some of the major killers are particles that form compounds in our air and water. These compounds in many cases are new, and no one knows their effect on the human body.

Air pollution can change climate and alter the shape of the continents. Some scientists argue that the climate is warming up, that the polar ice packs are melting and that one day we will be flooded. Others argue that it is getting colder, that a new ice age is on the way. Either way, they lay the blame on air pollution.

Pollution of the seas is changing the face of the continents. Where land masses have been protected by coral reefs, the reefs are dying. Reefs are built up by tiny microscopic animals that make shells out of calcium carbonate, or lime. It takes tens of thousands of years for reefs to build up on the shells of these tiny animals left as deposit after the animal has died. As the reefs die, the microorganisms die. Or, conversely, as the microorganisms die, the reef dies. The sea wears away the reefs. Then the barrier protecting the land from the sea is gone, and the land begins to wear away. In some places whole islands may be dying because the coral is so sensitive to changes in the chemical composition of the water and its temperature.

Nuclear power plants cause thermal pollution by heating lakes and streams with water that has been used to cool the plant. Fish and other aquatic animals and plants cannot stand sudden changes in water temperature. They die. and other forms of life take their places, altering the whole character of the body of water, sometimes for good but usually for the worse. Some attempt has been made to study the beneficial aspects of nuclear power plants, but aside from some large, fat and fast-growing turtles in Tennessee, little evidence of benefit has been found.

Estuaries, areas where fresh and salt water meet and mix, provide havens for some of the most beautiful birds, as well as other interesting forms of plant and animal life. Chemical fertilizers and pesticides are washing into the estuaries and on into the oceans, poisoning the food chains of these animals. The plants and the animals called zooplankton soak up the pesticides and nitrates, are eaten by baby fish, which are eaten by big fish, which are eaten by ospreys and pelicans, which can't hatch their eggs because DDT accumulation has made the shells so thin. In 1970 in California only one brown pelican egg was successfully hatched by its frantic parents, who, along with other birds, attempted four or five nestings. In the northeast, inland, it has recently been found that most male robins have been rendered sterile by pollution, and if something isn't quickly done they will join the passenger pigeon in the vast emptiness of extinction.

Rachel Carson made many people aware of the pesticide problem in her book *Silent Spring*. She waged a one-woman war against the chemical. Ralph Nader sees the warfare in broader terms. "Air pollution (and its fallout on soil and water) is a form of domestic chemical and biological warfare. The effluent from motor vehicles, plants, and incinerators of sulfur oxides, hydrocarbons, carbon monoxide, oxides of nitrogen, particulates and many more contaminants amounts to compulsory consumption of violence by most Americans. There is no full escape from such violent ingestions, for breathing is a necessity. This damage, perpetuated increasingly in direct violation of local, state, and federal law, shatters people's health and safety but still escapes inclusion in the crime statistics.

" 'Smogging' in a city or town has taken on the proportions of a massive crime wave, yet federal and state statistical compilations of crime pay attention to muggers and ignore 'smoggers.' As a nation which purports to apply law for preserving health, safety and property, there is a curious permissiveness toward passing and enforcing laws against the primary polluters who harm our society's most valued rights. In testament to the power of corporations and their retained attorneys, enforcement scarcely exists. Violators are openly flouting the laws and an Administration allegedly dedicated to law and order sits on its duties."

Air pollution eats away priceless works of art that survived for centuries before our time. Venice, London, New York, Los Angeles, and Florence are among the cities whose art treasures have been damaged by pollution. The figures on the cathedrals of these cities often have blurred features. They have to be cleaned every few years, a process which itself wears away even more of the precious carvings. Many art treasures have already been irreparably lost.

One of Ralph's task forces published a book called *The Vanishing Air* that is a compilation of horror stories. But the most horrible thing about them is that a modern city person can read them without feeling a thing. "What's so awful about that?" you say as you read. "We have that problem every day. What are they complaining about? Everyone knows you can't do anything about it."

It is precisely this public attitude, says Ralph, that has put us in the mess we are in. Corporations seem inpenetrable, but the fact is that they can easily be frightened. Their public images are concocted out of partial truths, and like the false fronts of buildings on Hollywood lots, they are easily destroyed.

A small town in West Virginia called Anmoore had a few valiant citizens who began to protest the fact that they literally ate, drank, and waded through the fly-ash from one of Union Carbide's plants near their town. The pollutants destroyed most of the vegetation in the area and affected the breathing of many of the town residents. Around the plant, the amount of ash and other substances in the air was five times that estimated to cause serious disease. In towns suffering such problems, the rise in allergies and other respiratory problems is astronomical.

In Houston, Texas, one can literally travel from smell to smell. An attempt to enforce an air pollution law was defeated when the key inspector-control posts were filled by industry men. The law itself is weak, but the enforcement of even its mild provisions is laughable.

New York is a major catastrophe. It has more pollution per person than any other city in the nation. It showed a 500 percent increase in emphysema between 1960 and 1972 and has one of the highest death rates from lung cancer in the country.

New York is saved to some extent by its prevailing winds. For the most part, there is enough wind to keep breathing bearable. But when the winds fail, as they often do, the city turns into a steaming cauldron of poisons. New York has a daily index of the quality of the air ranging from "good" to "unhealthy." The "good" days come rarely. Sometimes they are hopefully forecast only to become "unsatisfactory" by late afternoon. Eyes water, throats rasp, headaches pound in the sinuses. And some people who have trouble breathing stop breathing. Permanently.

New York has attempted to solve the problem wih laws forbidding the burning of high-sulfur-content fuels, which are a major cause of harmful pollutant compounds in the air, and upgrading incinerator requirements to keep particles out of the air. It also has instituted a series of graded alerts ranging from "forecast" to "emergency" and established the Department of Air Resources to administer the whole program.

The department has had its problems however. Its staff has been cut, and it examines only about 15 percent of the complaints it receives.

Residents of our cities unfortunately seem to think that because the air is tested every day something will be done about the danger to their health. Nothing could be further from the truth, Ralph Nader contends.

In the summer of 1971 New York, Tokyo and Sidney, Australia were all simultaneously blanketed under clouds of thick, unrelenting clouds of pollution. In New York, offices closed. In Tokyo, where gas masks are as common equipment for school children as their textbooks, the city virtually came to a halt. So did activities in Sidney. The pollution problems lasted different lengths of time and were totally unrelated, except that all were caused by man's misuse of his environment.

Despite warnings given in *The Vanishing Air* and other alarming articles in newspapers, magazines and consumer newsletters, very little of any consequence has been done to remedy the situation. President John-

111

son signed a clean air bill in 1967, yet the quality of the air has not markedly improved. The Department of Health, Education and Welfare has expressed concern. But will concern repair the lungs of an emphysema patient?

As Ralph sees it, there are two major factors. One is apathy. Apathy is a defense mechanism, but it can also be the result of laziness. Ralph understands the first but despises the second. He is continually after people to get off their chairs in front of the TV and do something, even if it is boycotting nonrecyclable materials and giving up cigarettes and the extra car. But people either cannot or, more likely, will not.

Industry has the same idea, but it is more calculated. "Sure," their attitude is, "we know that eventually raw materials will run out. But in the meantime we're going to make as much money as we can while they last, and to hell with the planet!"

The National Air Pollution Control Administration is the federal "mission" for air pollution control. It epitomizes the type of bureaucracy that is cynically regarded or ignored by many Americans.

Ralph regards it as a watchdog without teeth. "The deep loss of popular belief that government is capable of protecting and advancing public interest against this airborne epidemic and its corporate sources reflects a broader absence of confidence, particularly among the young, that government can be honest and courageous enough to administer law for the purpose."

NAPCA has a miniscule budget and staff, considering the task it has, yet Ralph's raiders found that it was not fighting for more money or staff. Even a congressional committee could not learn from its director exactly how much money he needed. They wanted to find out if he required more funds, but he was so evasive that they finally terminated the hearing in frustration.

Frustration, the raiders found, is the prevailing mood of the people who work for NAPCA—frustration, depression, and confusion. Everyone who works for the department knows how serious the situation is, but no one seems to know quite what to do.

Legislation, Ralph contends, has been puny and ineffectual. Although automobile manufacturers claim to have met standards set by the federal and local governments, the "tack on" devices to control emissions from exhausts have proven inadequate for the job. It is not, Ralph claims, that the industry does not know how to make a better, less-polluting car. It does not want to. It does not want to invest capital in such a project, and it does not want to raise its prices, because that would decrease sales and result in fewer cars on the road.

Automotive manufacturers' efforts at producing an alternative to the present type of car engine have in Ralph's view been laughable. Prototype steam engines and "electrovans" have been so obviously slapped together that they are wasteful in size and use of materials in proportion to the number of passengers they carry. Some are also highly dangerous, including one version that operates on a liquid hydrogen/oxygen fuel cell principle.

And yet GM built a lunar vehicle that was powered by solar energy, and it worked perfectly. Can we, Ralph asks, conclude that steam and other experimental cars are intentionally designed to discourage alternatives to the internal combustion engine?

Several alternative engines are already workable. A Wankel engine that works on a single-stroke principle with great efficiency has been installed in the back of a conventional European car (about half the size of most American cars). It works perfectly. Even some of the automobile giants in the United States have been forced to admit that a steam car does not have to look like a boiler on wheels, and that a steam unit can be installed in current model cars. Not only would this type of engine, called the Rankine Cycle, be nonpolluting, but it could be safer than engines currently in use, because damage from an accident could be a matter of water or steam tubes rupturing instead of highly flammable gas exploding.

In addition, the Rankine Cycle engine is simple, and it is very difficult to plan the obsolescence of a simple item. What would happen to the enormous profits gained from sales of replacement parts? And what would happen to the oil industry when the public began burning kerosene in their cars instead of expensive, much-refined gasoline? An electric engine would deal a heavy blow to the petroleum industry.

Up until 1970, the government, aided and abetted the automobile industry's foot-dragging. It allotted no funds for independent research on alternatives to the internal combustion engine. It simply passed laws and then waited for the industry to regulate itself or find its own alternatives. Amateurs have knocked together better models than Detroit has come up with, and every year, over the country, amateur clubs stage races, endurance contests and rallies based on the safety and nonpolluting qualities of their homemade cars. They are small in number, but their very presence is an embarrassment to General Motors, Ford, Chrysler and American Motors.

Ralph continues his investigation of the air pollution problem. He has attacked land development, strip mining practices, harmful pesticides and fertilizers, careless farm methods, inefficient rapid transit and other forms of pollution-related factors of daily life.

What remains now to be seen is whether the reform effort is too late . . . whether laws in existence will be enforced and new and tougher laws will be passed . . . whether the government will have the courage to defy the biggest corporations in America and stop them from killing their own consumers . . . whether government can be made to work again to safeguard the interests of its citizens.

CHAPTER
9

Nader's Raiders. It is a name that strikes terror in the hearts of some corporate executives, rage in others. It is a name that arouses hope in some and cynicism in others.

Who are the raiders and what do they do? How are they financed? What results have they achieved?

The nucleus of the organization is Ralph's public-interest law firm, the Public Interest Research Group (PIRG). Its members do not like to be called raiders, or even advocates. "We're trying to repair, to build," they say. They think of themselves as public citizens—professional citizens. Not all of them are lawyers. Some are economists and specialists in medicine, in engineering, and in other subjects related to current PIRG investigations. Most of them are young.

116

The term "raider" was coined because of Ralph's somewhat haphazard use of students to ferret out information. The girls from Miss Porter's School could hardly have been less experienced, yet they came up with the information that condemned the nursing home system and seriously questioned the quality of treatment of the aged. The students who investigated the Federal Food and Drug Adminstration and the food industry slept in tents off the Baltimore-Washington Parkway. They were paid a small salary for their summer's work—$500—yet they produced a prodigious amount of information and helped to focus the nation's attention on the dangers in the food industry and the laxity of the Food and Drug Administration.

Because of their guerrillalike tactics of appearing out of nowhere, gathering information, and then vanishing until they reappeared to testify at Congressional committee hearings, they acquired the name "raiders."

But as early as 1966 Ralph had begun to consider something more widespread and permanent than the early setup. Speaking at colleges, he urged students to organize their own PIRG's on campus with a dollar from each student.

The first "formal" group Ralph got together was the Center for Study of Responsive Law. He financed it with foundation grants and private donations. It was separate from the Task Force, which was also financed by foundations. It paid the students their summer fees and supplied them with guidance and with room and board.

Today, Ralph has fewer students and more profes-

117

sionals working for him. He still uses students on specific projects where he thinks they can do a better job, but working for Ralph is for the most part a tedious, long, exhausting and financially unrewarding job.

PIRG was funded by foundations and by the money that Ralph won in his suit against General Motors. It also receives donations from Ralph, whose income from speaking engagements (fee: $2,500 to $3,000), royalties from books, and other sources runs to nearly $200,000, according to some estimates. But he spends only $5,000 on himself per year. He lives modestly and sinks all his assets into PIRG and other projects.

His donors are a measure of Ralph's effectiveness. They range from anonymous citizens to business moguls. For example, Gordon Sherman, the head of the giant Midas Muffler empire, gives Ralph $100,000 a year. "I am in the amazing position of funding my own demise," he says. "Cars have to be summarily outlawed in the city. The automobile is obsolete." Here is a true Ralph Nader convert speaking the consumer gospel.

"My dream," Mr. Sherman says, "is to use the oil depletion allowance as a tax shelter to lobby against the oil depletion allowance and abolish it. I've discovered that there are many unused techniques whereby a man can give away vast amounts of money. But what I've also found is that people are afraid to give it away, not because they are greedy or selfish but because it's against the ethic. The middle class gives the money to itself: it gives to music and to hospitals or schools, which should be supported by the government because such things are noncontroversial."

It really is not strange, Mr. Sherman thinks, for a millionaire (and millionaires are notoriously stingy) to part company with his money for the Ralph Naders of the last half of the twentieth century. "In the final analysis we're doing it for ourselves," he says. "Businessmen are our last hope. We've gone through the clergy. The government is a hopeless sellout, so we businessmen are the last estate to put hope in."

And his opinion of Ralph? In one interview he was talking of him in conjunction with Saul Alinsky, the socialist organizer. "They're both trying to institutionalize and spread their ethic without enervating it. These men are lone, foraging geniuses."

Unfortunately, Gordon Sherman, a rebel in spirit with a businessman's practicality, is the exception to the general rule. He stands in sharp contrast to the usual attitude of "I'll take mine now, while it's still there." And he puts a lot of hope—"futile hope, maybe" —into what Ralph is doing.

Has Ralph succeeded in making his personal battle something that others can participate in? One of the members of PIRG put it this way. "Ralph puts a heavy burden on us. He expects us to have his stamina, his singleminded dedication. While many of us would feel the need to take a quick break, like a day in the mountains, when we're under particularly heavy fire, we don't do it. What would Ralph be doing? Maybe staying up for days and nights at a time, snatching an hour of sleep here or there. How can you go to the mountains with that on your conscience?"

Not that Ralph watches over his employees like a

119

hawk. "There was a time, in the beginning at the Center," a PIRG member says, "when there was a minor uprising among the staff. They complained that they never saw Ralph, that they didn't have enough guidance, that there was little camaradarie or team spirit.

"Ralph was hurt and confused by this. 'What do they want?' he asked. He simply didn't understand that all people are not made like him, a loner, obsessed with what he is doing to the exclusion of everything else. He said, 'They are working independently. They have freedom. I just don't understand it.' But the problem is that a lot of people can't take the freedom. It's a lonely business."

The lonely business goes on at all hours of the day and night. It is rarely glamorous. It involves reading the dullest technical journals, poring over the fine print of the *Congressional Record*, reading page after page of dull testimony, in order to find the few nuggets of information that may make or break a project. It means working all alone, with one's only comfort in knowing that there are others doing the same thing and that one can consult Ralph when he makes a whirlwind visit or else talk to other PIRG workers. It often means giving oneself a crash course in a highly technical field, such as the biochemistry of foods. It causes personal conflicts for some members, especially those who have families or are hoping to have them.

"Sometimes," says a PIRG worker, "even though you know how warm Ralph can be, you wonder about him. I want to take my kids to the marshes to look at the bird migrations, and then I think about Ralph's report lying on my desk waiting for me to finish it, and I have to choose between the kids and the public interest. I won't deny it causes problems. It does."

Yet there never seems to be a lack of people applying for the $4,500 starting salary. It seems incredible, but Ralph calls this low pay his screening program. "If they're willing to work for what I pay them, then they're genuinely interested. If they're not, then there are other places they can go." Ralph's employees are raised to the munificent sum of $9,000 (depending on how good their work is, and their financial need).

The amazing thing is that PIRG works. A graduate of Harvard Law School can always hope to land himself a well-paying position with a corporation, and often with a private law firm. Yet many law students choose to work with Ralph. It seems a poor financial reward, but most young law graduates claim that working on investigations involving corporations gives them inside knowledge into corporate workings that will prove invaluable later on. Not too many of Ralph's young associates are willing to admit it, but like Sherman Gordon, they think the corporations can only be changed by eventually having enough public citizens working inside them and applying pressure for change.

Nader's raiders come from a wide variety of backgrounds, but all share a common frustration at the impotence of government, its complicity in the cheating of the average consumer, and its disinterest in human welfare and safety. Like the hounds of heaven they pursue these disgraces relentlessly.

They have few illusions. Sometimes their cynicism

121

gets in their way. In *The Vanishing Air* they blasted Senator Edmund Muskie for being a sham conservationst, but failed to mention that he proposed legislation in 1970 to fine air pollutors $50,000 a day along with prison sentences. Although some congressmen and senators propose legislation they never expect to see passed, just to please their constituents, Senator Muskie's efforts were regarded by most observers as sincere.

Nader's workers feel they have a lot to learn about the painstaking kind of investigating that is essential to PIRG. "Ralph is a fantastic teacher," says one of the members. "When he's here, he's really *with* you. He doesn't waste time; he's teaching every single minute. You drink it in. And you remember it. If you make a mistake, you feel horrible about it. There's no one to blame but yourself, because you don't report to anyone but Ralph himself. Ralph calls it a bureaucracy, but it isn't that at all. It's too honest and direct, and you know where you stand all the time. If you produce, you know you'll be kept on. If you don't, you probably want out anyway."

Another former raider puts it this way. "Ralph makes you grow up. And you've got to be at your most mature every second; otherwise you'll get caught, laughed at, and ignored. There isn't any time for play. Usually the material is leading to something that affects life and limb, health and safety. It's serious business, and while we do laugh it's usually gallows humor and to the point."

"There isn't any doubt that Ralph has charisma," says

another former raider. "You're slogging along, maybe getting depressed, and in walks this incredible human being who treats himself like a machine. Somehow that makes things easier . . . I don't know why he has such presence. He's entirely opposite to the popular image of someone who has achieved fame and fortune. He doesn't flash a $10,000 smile, and he rarely says anything that doesn't pertain to the business at hand. But when he does start it, it takes a long time before he's finished."

"Working for Ralph gives you a feeling of power," states another. "You walk into someone's office, and you can almost see him sweat. It isn't a nice feeling, though. It's rather frightening. Many corporations are running scared, and the officer you talk to knows that not only his job but also the stock of the company, and maybe the company itself, is on the line. The same is true in the government offices. They have stories to tell you about why you can't see such and such a file or statement. It gets to the point of absurdity, especially when you know that the statement appeared in a national magazine and all you have to do is go to one of the wire services. But they just don't want to give us anything they have."

Recently, PIRG has entered a new phase. It has gone public. In full page ads in newspapers and magazines across the country, and by direct mail Ralph is soliciting funds for PIRG on the basis of "professional citizenship."

From his first advertisement in *The New York Times* Ralph made a profit of about $45,000. He continued to

What can just one private citizen do?

Ralph Nader urges you to become a Public Citizen

Dear Fellow Citizen:

Imagine that 25 or 30 years ago citizens concerned about the future quality of life in America had gotten together to do something about it.

Suppose they had begun an effective citizen's campaign to make government agencies and industry management sensitive and responsive to the needs of the people. The *real* needs, of *all* the people.

Think how much that was already wrong would have been corrected by now.

Think how much that has gone wrong since then would never have been allowed to happen.

In another 30 years our population will have doubled. What if our rampant economic "growth" is allowed to continue indiscriminately—mindless of the public's hopes and indifferent to their problems?

What if we continue to do nothing because we assume that others are taking care of the problems and fears that plague us?

Who *is* taking care of them?

It is clear that our institutions, public and private, are not really performing their regulatory functions. They tend not to control power democratically, but to concentrate it and to serve special interest groups at the expense of voiceless citizens.

Almost all the organized legal representation in our country is working to protect private interests and private wealth.

Who represents the citizen? Only ourselves. And that is why I urge you, as a public citizen—a citizen concerned about your community and your country—to support Public Citizen.

Thousands of graduates of law, medical, science and engineering schools and other disciplines want to work long hours, at minimal wages in the public interest. They know that our society cannot solve its problems if all our most highly trained professionals work for private industry or government agencies.

If these selfless young people are willing to sacrifice conventional rewards to pioneer the future, other public spirited citizens will surely want to make it possible for them to do so.

Through Public Citizen, we ask you to contribute $15 to support a lean, hard-working group of these citizen-advocates.

Through published studies and documentation, they will help to sharpen public awareness of our problems. Public awareness leads to public action.

They will represent disadvantaged minority groups, including students, before the various legal agencies of state and federal governments. They will seek to temper the actions of large corporations that have acquired power far out of proportion to their contributions to society.

In some important way, every major company touches on the lives of thousands of people—employees, consumers, retailers, taxpayers and whole communities. Shouldn't these people have a voice about policies that directly, adversely affect them? Must not a just legal system accord victims the ability to deter forces that tend to victimize them?

A way must be found to make a real impact on corporate boardrooms—and on government agencies that often serve as protectors, even service arms, of industries they are supposed to regulate.

Bureaucrats cannot easily resist the overwhelming pressures of special interest lobbies in Washington and state capitals. But there can be a greater countervailing pressure—the determination of citizens lobbying for the public interest.

Once a year, as a Public Citizen supporter, you will receive a report on significant new citizen involvements that have been effective in achieving reform or relief at the local, state, or national level. Hopefully, you will apply them in the areas of your own commitment to action. Citizenship skills must be continually sharpened and used if we are to succeed in preventing or diminishing injustice.

Potentially, there are 200 million of us unable to work full-time for the public interest but with a full-time anxiety about it. Think how much can be accomplished if enough private citizens become *public citizens*.

Please mail the coupon and your check for $15 or more to help Public Citizen continue and expand the work that is already under way.

Let it not be said by a future, forlorn generation that we wasted and lost our great potential because our despair was so deep we didn't even try, or because each of us thought someone else was worrying about our problems.

Sincerely,

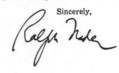

Public Citizen, Inc. P.O. Box 19404
Washington, D.C. 20036

I am a Public Citizen. Here's my $15.00 (I enclose an additional $_____). Please don't waste any of it sending me a membership card or literature. I know what's wrong. What I want is to see something done about it.

Name _____

Address _____

City _____ State _____ Zip _____

Please make check payable to: Public Citizen, Inc.

run the ads and continually appeals to private individuals and foundations for support.

Ralph's groups, especially the center for the Study of Responsive Law and PIRG, have not gone without difficulties. Ralph has gained and lost good friends and excellent workers. Jim Turner, head researcher and writer for *The Chemical Feast*, left after differences with Ralph and is continuing to work in the field in the midwest. Ralph also has difficulty finding enough satisfactory people to consider for "permanent" places in PIRG. Three percent is a generous estimate of the number of people accepted out of thousands of applicants. For every hundred who apply, three are judged to be able, and even then there is some attrition.

Nevertheless, the groups have produced a formidable array of reports. Among them, besides *The Vanishing Air*, *The Chemical Feast*, and the report on nursing homes, there is *The Interstate Commerce Omission* and *Citibank*. *The Interstate Commerce Omission* is a blast at the Interstate Commerce Commission attacking its status as the government's regulatory agency; hence the tongue-in-cheek title. It points out that the commission is a virtual cartel, controlled by a group of businessmen in the transportation field dedicatedly looking after their own interests and deciding their own rates. *Citibank* is a report on the second-largest bank in the United States. There also is a report on the Department of Agriculture, and a report on the Army Corps of Engineers and its destruction of land, resources and wilderness areas by unnecessary damming and waterworks projects. There are reports on drugs, gas and pipelines, mine safety, and at least ten other vital problems.

But Ralph warns us that the years since 1966 have been a mere warm-up. An investigation of the Congress of the United States has begun. "Audacious?" exclaims Ralph in response to a question, "You bet it's audacious. When the country learns just how weak Congress is, how a few men control a body of several hundred representatives, how the committee and seniority systems preserve the status quo, and political favors are traded for human lives, there could quite well be a citizens' revolt!"

No doubt the investigation of Congress will lead to studies of the Pentagon, the Supreme Court, the United States Treasury Department, and perhaps even the presidency. There is no telling. Ralph believes that a large part of the problem with society lies in government: waste, footdragging, lack of appropriations to enforce the laws in effect, payoffs and other corruption, nepotism and a host of skeletons in federal closets.

PIRG is not working alone. Ralph's current structure of organizations looks something like the chart opposite.

Ralph wants to involve as many people as possible in his crusade for a better life for Americans, and he does not care whom he alienates.

"Sure," says one raider, "a lot of people hate us. The liberals hate us because we steal their thunder. They talk big and do little. 'White man speak with forked tongue,' as the old saying goes. The corporate establishment hates us because we destroy their carefully groomed images. Even a lot of housewives hate us be-

126

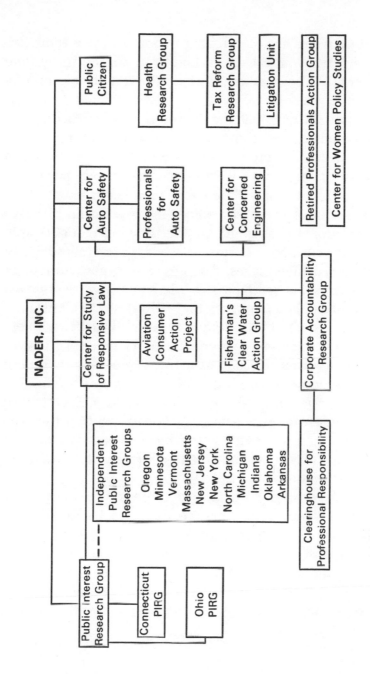

cause we're always bugging people to leave their kaffeeklatches and TV sets and crap games and get to work. We're gadflies. We could even start a revolution."

But can and will they? Americans are famous for their apathy and short attention span. Will the American people become bored with PIRG, the Center and all of Ralph Nader's works once the novelty wears off?

"I don't think so," says a former raider from one of the original volunteer offices in New York. "PIRG is exposing new elements all the time. Sure, it's scratching the surface in some ways, but it's scratching in the most sensitive places. Enough so that government or the courts at least have to do some investigation on their own. You might say that PIRG and the Center are like those obnoxious people at cocktail parties who enjoy stepping into a conversation and beginning a discussion, and then, as soon as it turns into an acrimonious debate, quietly slipping away, thoroughly enjoying the knowledge that they have done it again. Society and the industrial establishment, not to mention the government, is so complex and harbors so many horrors that the groups will be able to offer new hors d'oeuvres every year.

"I'm not so sure about these grassroot groups, though," he goes on. "People, thanks to Auntie Madison Avenue, think their right is leisure and jet-set living— or at least a quiet beer while they watch the tube in their undershirts or housedresses. Not all of America— maybe not even five percent of the legal profession— are Naders. In fact, I know only one Nader: Ralph. He's

128

broken up marriages with his 3 A.M. phone calls, but I still haven't found anyone like him. God knows what we'd do if the candle burning at both ends and in the middle burned out."

Another raider who quit working for Ralph said, "I'm not ashamed that I left the Center. I was idealistic, and I needed to get it out of my system, not that I've dropped those values. I haven't. But I found out that I could carry on the sort of work that led me to Ralph in the first place in my own way. It takes all kinds of people, you know, to get something across. And not only by being a full-time lawyer for the Center or PIRG. It's like fighting a war, or converting people to a religion. The reason Ralph's been able to do what he's done is his example. Well, you need examples in other fields besides law, and in other places besides Washington. It's got to be a groundswell, not a fashion from the top."

Religion is the right word for it. Because what Ralph ultimately hopes for is a whole new way for Americans to think about life, business, government, manners and morals—a viewpoint that suffuses every aspect of society. He sees a culture disintegrating around him ("It's like the fall of the Roman Empire"), and he believes he knows what must be done to save it. And despite what some critics say, he seems to think it is worth saving. But to do so we must act as if there is an emergency— because there is.

A lot of people have said that Ralph Nader is hopelessly naive in that he really believes it is possible to change human nature. Perhaps he is, but a growing number of respectable observers besides Ralph Nader have solemnly stated that something as drastic as that may be the only hope the world has for survival. The greed that has created the profits-before-safety attitude of many industries is typical of human nature—and the resulting pollution may wipe out the human race. The vanity and power-lust that provoke nations to outdo each other in the size of armies and weapons, and to set those armies and weapons upon one another—that's human nature, too, and the resulting nuclear cataclysm may destroy the planet. The envy that has made every nation on earth want to live as well as the most opulent countries in existence—that's human nature, and the resulting plunder of the earth's resources may exhaust them forevermore.

The greatest sages and prophets in history did little to change human nature. But now the imperative points at our heads like a gun: change and survive, or don't change and risk the Day of Reckoning.

CHAPTER
10

Just who is Ralph Nader anyway? Or who does he think he is?

His critics have a lot to say. "He's a scold." "He's a Don Quixote, tilting at windmills." "He's inhuman, cold, emotionless." "He's ruining American business and the way we live." "He's embarked on a program that will lead to nothing but folly." "He's being paid by the Reds." "Arrogant, unfeeling, presumptuous." "He's a facist, socialist, anarchist, dictator."

These are, for the most part, hysterical charges. But there is some valid criticism of Nader.

One of the biggest criticisms of Ralph is that he overestimates the people working for him or underestimates the people he attacks. Once he trusts someone, he trusts him implicitly. This sometimes puts him out

131

on a limb. When he accepted the reports of some raiders who had gone to California to research a campaign against destructive land development, his speeches were full of factual errors. He accused one of *Fortune*'s top 500 companies of gross misuse of land in Hawaii. That corporation, grumped the *San Francisco Chronicle* the next day, had never constructed a building there, owned a piece of land there, or even been in Hawaii in any way as a corporate entity.

That kind of error can be devastating to the Nader cause, yet Ralph continues to rely on raiders' reports. He could not possibly function otherwise.

Ralph's overestimation of his followers blinds him, and occasionally he feels let down. He finds it hard to understand how any raider or member of PIRG would drink liquor, smoke, drink coffee, eat processed food—how could they, after all the reports? He assumes their lifestyles follow his: hence the 3 A.M. telephone calls.

On the other hand, he often underestimates his antagonists.

Another serious charge leveled at Ralph is that his groups are beginning to resemble the very bureaucracies he is attacking. They are large and unwieldy and hard to control. They are, say his critics, becoming establishments in themselves, setting up standards for the quality of life in a self-justifying manner. Sometimes, instead of arousing sympathy, he arouses resentment. "Who is this guy who thinks he can tell me what to do?" This attitude was very much in evidence when cyclamates were taken off the market. People depended on the noncaloric sweeteners, and some people bought up

132

stocks of soft drinks to lay away for future consumption.

Seatbelts and shoulder harnesses have suffered a similar fate, and so has much of the other legislation that has been passed since Ralph came on the scene. Except for the Traffic and Motor Vehicle Safety Act, which can hardly be called a failure with over 7 million cars recalled in the first four months of 1972, few of the bills—the Clean Air Act, the Coal Mine Health and Safety Act, the Federal Meat Inspection Act, the Natural Gas Pipeline Safety Act—have achieved even modest improvements in the areas they were designed to regulate. In short, they have failed in that they have not changed anything radically.

Yet Ralph does not regard himself as a failure. "I knew the bills would fail. I said when the Traffic and Motor Vehicle Safety act was passed that we'd see few effects before 1975, and the rate's been slower for truly crashproof cars than even I had thought." Ralph knew the other bills would fail, too. Partly because they were watered down by powerful lobbies. But he does not think the whole enterprise has been a failure, because, if nothing else, the failure of the bills lays the blame at government's door: state, federal and local. Congress allocates inadequate funds. Government hires insufficient, even token, personnel to enforce acts. Perhaps it is all a farce, as some say, but at least now it is an exposed farce.

Perhaps in the area of legislative effectiveness Ralph can be called a failure. But it is nothing short of miraculous that a solitary man in our success-oriented society can stand up to failure of this magnitude and keep going. Ralph is sometimes subject to despair, but he plods on, charting a steady course through killing twenty-hour days.

Ralph can hardly be called a failure in his personal crusade to effect change. His intensely private life and utter integrity have set him head-and-shoulders above any popular leader who has emerged in the last two decades. He claims he will never run for office. This remains to be seen. He stays out of politics for the most part, but his work is essentially political, for to make the changes he sees as crucial to the human and national survival, one must play politics to a great extent. He deals with politicians constantly, yet he has maintained his image as essentially nonpolitical. He does not work for anyone but himself and for the people.

What do Ralph Nader and his work add up to? It is really too early to evaluate what the long-term effects will be, but some of the short-term effects are obvious.

Someone once said that Ralph has a "Founding-Father complex." In spite of his battle with the corporate establishment he is very much in favor of an establishment where law and order reign ("Not a police state," says Ralph), where productivity is in line with prices and profits, where corporate honesty and fair dealing are common practices, and where science and technology are harmoniously balanced with nature and with human needs.

The Pilgrim fathers came to the New World to escape religious persecution. Now the persecution is technological. Ralph's idea of professional citizenship includes not only active participation in local PIRGs but increased sensitivity to our fellow man. The citizen must not only "fight City Hall"; he must fight the values that made City Hall the way it is, thus making citizenship and the vote mean something again.

The early settlers of this country were heroes, though they did not think of themselves as such. Ralph Nader has recaptured some of their spirit. There are few geographic frontiers to conquer now, but exploration of the complex corridors of corporations and government has just begun.

Ralph is fond of haranguing his college audiences. "It's your world," he will say. "You'd better plan on doing something about it now, or there won't be anything left.

The college audiences listen. Though easily bored, they sit through two-hour lectures. And they volunteer. There is something in Ralph Nader that makes people want to participate. He requires them to be adults, to take the responsibility for a world that might not be there tomorrow. Ironically, Ralph finds many youth more mature than the people running the corporations and agencies.

Although the PIRG offices are inhabited by people wearing casual styles, there is no doubt in anyone's mind about their motivations—the reestablishment of such out-of-date values as peace, harmony, and honesty, the very principles of the American dream.

"When you consider," said one very dry humorist, "what the country is made of, it's a miracle we survived at all. Gentry and indentured servants, and then masses of people. Just look at the inscription on Miss Liberty:

135

'Give me your tired, your poor, your huddled masses yearning to breathe free, the restless refuse of your teeming shores. . . .' Whoever heard of building anything but cheap housing on a refuse heap?"

Ralph may superficially resemble a Mayflower personality, but nothing like him has ever existed before, and nothing like the society he envisions has ever existed before, either. He may not be able to change human nature but he can change human attitudes. He already has. Radically.